the art
of confession

the art of confession

Renewing Yourself Through the Practice of Honesty

Paul Wilkes

WORKMAN PUBLISHING • NEW YORK

For my beloved Tracy, for whom honesty is unnervingly natural

Library of Congress Cataloging-in-Publication Data is available.

ISBN 978-0-7611-5596-6

Workman books are available at special discounts when purchased in bulk for premiums and sales promotions as well as for fund-raising or educational use. Special editions or book excerpts also can be created to specification. For details, contact the Special Sales Director at the address below or send an e-mail to specialmarkets@workman.com.

Jacket design: Jean-Marc Troadec
Interior design: Janet Vicario with Andi Paul

Workman Publishing Company, Inc.
225 Varick Street
New York, NY 10014-4381
www.workman.com

Printed in the United States of America

First printing December 2011

10 9 8 7 6 5 4 3 2 1

Acknowledgments

Deepest thanks to two exacting and
excellent editors, Ruth Sullivan and Savannah Ashour;
to Peter Workman, who championed the idea;
and to my agent, John Thornton.

"A lie has speed. But truth has endurance."
—Edgar J. Mohn

"The soul would have no rainbow
Had the eyes no tears."
—John Vance Cheney

"To become acquainted with oneself means also to
understand preconsciously that the limits of our emotional
life are drawn upward and downward much farther
than we thought. This means, conventionally speaking,
that we are unconsciously much more wicked, but also
much better than we thought we were."
—Theodor Reik,
THE COMPULSION TO CONFESS

contents

introduction

We are at liberty to be real, or to be unreal. We may
be true or false, the choice is ours. We may wear now
one mask and now another, and never, if we so desire,
appear with our own true face. But we cannot make these
choices with impunity. Causes have effects, and if we lie
to ourselves and to others, then we cannot expect to find
truth and reality whenever we happen to want them.
If we have chosen the way of falsity we must not be
surprised that truth eludes us when we finally come
to need it!

—*Thomas Merton*

DEEP WITHIN EVERY human heart, there is the
desire to be good.

That is the core assumption of this book. We all
want to find and be our best selves, to go to bed each night at
peace with who we are and how we acted that day. We want

to be the kind of person we ourselves would want as a friend: trustworthy, dependable, fair. Yet often we fail—ourselves and others—in ways both small and significant.

This universal desire has a quiet yet perceptible voice: It is our conscience, a mysterious force within that urges us toward good actions and away from the bad. Having a free will means we can choose to listen to this voice or not. As we have all experienced, we can deflect or even blunt our conscience and choose to act in ways that are not in keeping with our best selves. And we know the vague, disquieting feeling, or sometimes the overwhelming sensation, when we do this.

What can lift this burden and restore our humanity is confession, a word that will be used often on these pages. In my religious tradition, Catholicism, the word "Confession" has a very specific meaning. That is not what we will explore here. Instead, we will be looking at confession with a small *c*. This sort of confession may be directed to a higher power, but it is first and foremost a conversation with ourselves. In other words, you don't have to walk into a church to cleanse your soul. This book is not so much about public confession as it is about private honesty.

Confession, as we will see later, is at the very foundation of all the great faiths and spiritual disciplines. All honor its power and have addressed the need for personal confession.

Confession is also a pillar of mental health, for confession is about self-examination. It demands something for which there is no substitute: that we be honest with ourselves.

Confession strips away the veil that we often cast over our actions, realigning our souls with what is best and truest in our natures. I use the word "align," because when we betray ourselves (some would define this as sinning), we fall out of alignment. Until we acknowledge—confess—our souls remain confused and fragmented.

This kind of confession, which demands self-reflection and change, has little to do with the flood of confessional disclosures that characterize our age—on tell-all TV talk shows and social networking sites, even via an iPhone app for confession. In this time of Internet connectivity, amid the din of oversharing, we mistake spasms of self-revelation for honesty. Our inner voice is not so easily found and cannot be parsed into ten-second bursts. That voice needs time to find the right words to say and the right place to say them.

Because it has been so trivialized, confession has lost its power and vitality. To confess is considered foolish, weak, even corrosive to our self-esteem, unnecessary. "Such an antiquated notion," some might say, "of right and wrong. What a naive understanding of how things really work, what people are really like."

The truth is that confession, as I seek to redefine it in this book, is wise and strong and necessary, unburdening both the soul and the psyche to live a forthright, productive, and fuller life. Confession is not only for those who have committed some great public or private "sin." For most of us, our "little murders"—our duplicities, the daily hurts, neglects, and carelessness we inflict upon others and upon ourselves—need to be confronted and acknowledged.

When confession becomes a practice, a daily reevaluation of one's actions—an art—its power continues to grow, instilling a new sense of confidence, a vision of what life truly can be and hold. Something as simple as a short, nightly *examen,* which I'll discuss in chapter 5, can sort out the chaff from the wheat of the day, clearing the mind right then, and inculcate a habit of living an examined life.

Although the word seems to indicate it, confession is not about guilt. (Though I would argue that a certain amount of guilt is good and necessary, as it helps to regulate moral behavior.) Nor is confession about wallowing in one's shortcomings, stupid mistakes, even our most horrific actions.

A Massachusetts parish priest once told me, "People who come to me confessing their faults and asking for help in dealing with life's problems often say, 'I don't know how to cope with this; help me learn a skill. I don't like who I am;

I want to be a better person.' People may not use those exact words, but that's what they are saying. They know they are better than the sum of their mistakes."

Using confession to live honestly and consciously—the goal in this book—is an art to be learned and a skill to be practiced. It is neither an easy fix nor a heal-all. Our brash modern optimism assumes that all can be made well if we only will it to be so, but human behavior is complex, requiring deeper thought and actual, sometimes painful recalibration.

Confession is, quite simply, an attitude. It is the cornerstone of the intentional life, not merely a clearing out of the debris, that which is bad or wrong in us, but a realignment of what is best in us, an intention to live a better life. It is building upon something strong and sure and ultimately reliable. Confession is about truth, and as Thomas Merton writes in the epigraph, what follows from an attitude of truth will not fail us.

MEET THE CONFESSIONAL CHORUS

THROUGHOUT THE CHAPTERS in this book you will find sidebars about confession from a rabbi, a priest, a psychiatrist, and a Roman Catholic nun who "ministers" in a bookstore. Here are their stories:

Rabbi Robert Waxman of B'nai Israel Synagogue in my hometown of Wilmington, North Carolina, is a compact man with a quizzical smile and a short beard. Rabbi Waxman's expression of religious belief is Judaism's middle road, the Reconstructionist movement, which embraces some of the dietary and ritual practices of the Orthodox with the tempering influences of Reform Judaism. He is married to a college professor and has two grown children.

Father Steven LaBaire has been a parish priest in the diocese of Worcester, Massachusetts, for more than twenty-five years. He is over fifty years old but looks younger, with long, brown hair that he wears in a vaguely 1950s style. He has heard thousands of confessions, both the traditional variety—called the Sacrament of Reconciliation—and informal ones in his office or in his home, a few steps from the church of St. Mary's in Uxbridge, where he is the pastor.

Dr. Thomas Mathew is a psychiatrist born in India, educated in England, and now practicing in the United States. He is tall, over six one, with a steady, attentive gaze. His Trinity Wellness Center in Wilmington, North Carolina, combines the mind-body-spirit approach once looked down upon by the psychiatric community but now a popular model. Dr. Mathew might recommend talk therapy, medication, yoga, or other regimes. He is married, with three young children.

Sister Karen Kirby is a Roman Catholic nun who chooses to exercise her ministry in the Well Spring Catholic Bookstore in Dayton, Ohio. A member of the Congregation of Saint Joseph, Sister Karen has the kind of open, animated, friendly face that first invites conversation and then allows it, taking on the look of a concerned friend that you have known for years—even though you may have been in the store for only a few minutes.

a confessional culture

Apology Versus Confession

WE ARE A CONFESSIONAL nation, with people ready, even eager to tell of their failings—failings that a generation or two ago we would have taken equal effort to conceal. Infidelity, addiction, collapses in our relationships with family and friends, even criminal acts—all are grist for the confession mill.

Over drinks with friends, we glibly announce that we are having an affair, no longer love our spouses, aren't sure we ever did—the cheating was inevitable, we say, even positive in helping us discover ourselves. What can you do? we ask, reaching for our martini, the writing was on the wall.

In chat rooms filled with strangers, people of all ages and walks of life share their darkest and loneliest secrets—struggles with eating disorders, substance abuse, compulsions, betrayals. They seek acceptance, community, absolution—though they would never call it by that name— for they have done nothing wrong but have simply "acted out," ruffling the feathers of convention and bruising a few feelings along the way. A studio audience on a daytime talk show cheers the honesty of our revelation, applauds our tears. We do not weep alone; they weep with us. Their support seems so intimate and personal, yet as we draw back, we realize how generic and impersonal it is.

There's been much written about how the electronic age, with its constant influx of data, affects our relationships, our stress levels, our attention spans. But little has been said about how the ease with which we hit the Share button may affect us on an even deeper level. We share to release, commune, commiserate. But we do it unconsciously, in an adrenaline-emboldened flash of the moment, without intention or reflection.

Something is missing. There is a hollowness to our supposed honesty. The purifying effects, the release of what used to be called "coming clean," are strangely absent. Hannah Arendt told how the "banality of evil" became a norm in Nazi Germany. Could it be that we have entered a time when the "banality of guilt" has so dulled our sense of right and wrong that we blithely admit offenses against others and ourselves without ever really, in the popular phrase, "taking responsibility for our actions," never feeling the need to take corrective measures so as not to repeat those offenses? Is the pointer on our inner compass so bent, our inner gyro so unstable, that we can no longer reset our path through life?

As individuals, as a culture, we seem to be in some moral free fall. "Social norms, the invisible threads that guide human behavior, have deteriorated," writes David Brooks in *The New York Times.* The institutions that used to help us recalibrate—government, church, family—seem unable to right themselves. They are neither as stable nor as blameless as we once hoped or believed. The Catholic church's failure to confront the evils of sexual abuse by its clergy is just one startling example. In less dramatic ways, for the religious and nonreligious of all stripes, social cohesion has worn away. Many writers and philosophers have pointed to the absence of a shared set of values as the cause of a postmodern, pervasive sense of isolation and anxiety. The causes are various, but the end result is the same: We are ultimately alone with our daily guilts, big and small.

LIGHTS, CAMERA, CONFESSION

If we have mixed feelings about the efficacy and place of confession these days, it is in no small part due to the parade of political figures who "confessed" their failings in public. President Bill Clinton vehemently denied but then was forced to admit indiscretions with a White House aide. Eliot Spitzer, the governor of New York, eventually admitted his liaisons with a prostitute; John Edwards, with a campaign aide; and preacher Ted Haggard, with another man. Cardinal Bernard Law of Boston was forced to admit that he allowed pedophile priests to be transferred from parish to parish, even after he knew they had molested children.

But these public "confessions" neither satisfied the public nor reached the level of honesty that integrity demands. In 2007, *Time* magazine weighed in on the subject of political malfeasance with an essay entitled "The Confession Procession": "In politics, as in church, there's no telling when penitence is sincere, for God alone knows the human heart. But it's a useful test in judging character to ask whether admitting failure comes at a cost—or a discount."

In *The Art of the Public Grovel,* Susan Wise Bauer further delineates this useful distinction: "An apology is an expression of regret: *I am sorry.* A confession is an admission of fault: *I am sorry because I did wrong. I sinned.*" Apology addresses an audience. Confession implies an inner change, a new understanding that will be manifested in outward action. What the politicians served up were apologies, not confessions—troubling, infuriating half measures, calculatingly phrased as self-defense.

The Quest for Catharsis

Major public figures have their arena, but we ordinary sinners have not been left out of the confession procession. It's not difficult to see the potential for shallowness in a television, print, or online confession, but there must be some benefit. Why else would anyone risk such a public display? A few may derive exhibitionistic satisfaction, but most, I believe, are simply compelled to tell the truth about their lives. Something is wrong. They want to make it right. They have made mistakes and desperately tried to forget or hide them; those mistakes haunt them.

Unless confession leads to a deeper understanding of why we did what we did and, far more important, how we can come into a truer alignment with what is best in us, we may achieve a moment's relief but no real change. We have put a small patch over a deeper wound. Our demons will visit again, often with worse consequences.

If we believe the only benefit of confession to be

catharsis, we underestimate its potential power. One part of confession is like exhaling, expelling air that is useless in sustaining life. This is the telling—in whatever way we do it—of our faults and failings. But just as our bodies naturally follow each exhalation with an inhalation, taking in the fresh, life-giving air, there is another part to confession, offering its true vitality.

If confession can be understood as an emptying to make room for something better (and, as we will discuss, a continual practice of honesty), it holds far more for us. That is, *if* we are willing to give up supposed innocence and self-defense, *if* we are willing to honestly take stock of ourselves and then (though this is neither easy nor quick) change how we live our lives.

The Battle for Being

In my early days as a reporter, I did many stories on celebrities. As I sat there with pad and pen, listening, I was often puzzled by the conflicting, shifting shards of the lives I was trying to piece together. Could these movie stars, elected officials, or wealthy industrialists still tell apart their personas from their real selves?

I remember doing a story for *The New York Times Magazine* on the famous criminal lawyer F. Lee Bailey. I saw him perform masterfully in the courtroom, dazzling and amusing his admirers with his witty answers and asides. It was quite a show, but in the course of watching it, I slowly came to the realization that everything was negotiable to him. Truth and untruth were functions of necessity. He was whoever he needed to be, depending on the situation. Each day existed as if there had been no yesterday and there would be no tomorrow. I felt as if he was writing a script for a character, a caricature, rather than responding, speaking, acting as a sentient being. It was one of the most frightening experiences of my life.

As for me, personally, at that time, I remember so well walking the streets of Greenwich Village, a man in his prime who, by the world's standards, had everything: A fabulous apartment on one of the best blocks. A television talk show and series. Invitations to A-list parties along with Kurt Vonnegut and Andy Warhol. An address book that brimmed with the names and phone numbers of lovely young women. Tailor-made clothes from the most fashionable Madison Avenue shops.

But behind the facade of supposed happiness, my life was purposeless—I had devoted it only to my own pleasures. I had lost my bearings, lost the art of conscious living instilled by my parents—the son and daughter of poor immigrants, believers in honesty, fairness, concern for others. I wasn't evil, but I was fooling myself that my pointless life really did have meaning, that "instant intimacy" was a true and honest emotion instead of a pathetic excuse to short-circuit normal human interactions in order to satisfy the need of the moment.

I can still recall the debilitating panic I felt whenever I let my guard down. I couldn't breathe. I thought I would collapse. I felt disoriented. It was horrible and so frightening that I would immediately seek refuge in whatever person or pleasure I could quickly find.

Jewish philosopher Martin Buber, one of the true sages of the twentieth century, would have described my condition as part of the death of *being* and the rise of *seeming:* "The widespread tendency to live from the recurrent impression one makes instead of from the steadiness of one's being . . . To yield to seeming is man's essential cowardice, to resist it is his essential courage. . . . One must at times pay dearly for the life lived from the being; but it is never too dear."

We have certainly smoothed off the rough, annoying edges of morality, domesticated the frightening consequences of the sins of dishonesty, cheating, lust, selfishness—the entire panoply of human failings. But there's no doing away with the destabilizing effects of our personal duplicity. We can blame Dr. Freud and therapy or, more recently, our television preachers who relentlessly point toward bluer skies, even as our moral clouds hover overhead. Self-improvement is all. It is not so ironic that the cross is absent from so many megachurches. It is we who are at center stage; we are the hallowed ones; of what use is this reminder of suffering?

It was only when I spent a year as a hermit, away from this life and this person I had become but could hardly recognize, that I could see I had been *seeming.* It was only when I looked at my actions honestly that I slowly, painfully began to change them—with the help of a therapist, God, prayer, and the woman who would eventually become my wife.

I no longer wanted to *seem* to be a person neither I nor God knew. Instead, I reached back into my life and found who I was—and could be again, older and, I hoped, wiser. By honest and constant reflection on my daily actions, I could—would—be a husband and father, two roles that I'd thought would condemn me to an ordinariness I feared. Instead I found the meaning I hadn't known I'd sought. I could *be,* and if that was ordinary, then I was.

Confession, or a confessional mind-set, isn't only for those who struggle with deep, gnawing secrets or even only

From Dr. Thomas Mathew

THE LOST ART OF SELF-EXAMINATION

I think one of the great dilemmas of our age is that we are walking about in a daze much of the time. We dull ourselves with recreational drugs like alcohol, with the busyness we heap upon ourselves with iPhones and overloaded schedules, with anything so that we are not forced to take stock of who we are, what we are doing with our lives, to what purpose, where this is all going.

We have such a blurred, distorted image of decisions. Some are just decisions—for instance, choosing what kind of sandwich to have for lunch. But there are others that need to be considered, important decisions about what is right and what is wrong.

We are confused in those decisions because we have either lost or sublimated—buried, really—the art of self-examination. Self-examination cannot exist when we continue to act on impulses and have so much going on that we don't have a moment to really think, think deeply.

for those who regularly undertip or overindulge. It is also for those whose being has been eclipsed by seeming.

We need honest self-reflection and self-appraisal. We can summon this sort of confession; our deepest self seeks it.

BETWEEN GUILT AND
NO-FAULT MORALITY

In the not-so-distant past, guilt and shame were popular, powerful, and oft-used moral forefingers that kept us in line as children. When we did something wrong, parents, teachers, neighbors, and the media images that also shaped us formed an unassailable moral bulwark. No compromise. No excuses.

Contrast this with today's drip-dry, no-fault morality, which coos that no one should be ashamed of anything, that there is a good excuse for any behavior, and that to linger on our shortcomings is self-defeating and unnecessary. Neither of these two approaches to life, practiced without understanding and introspection, promise to shape a healthy, honest, happy human being or provide the moral fiber necessary for the functioning of a civil society, a marriage, a family.

The film *Revolutionary Road* is a searing portrait of two people unable to be honest with themselves in their dying marriage. A line from the film is haunting: "No one forgets the truth; they just get better at lying." The answer for us is not to become more practiced at lying but to reach for the truth deep within ourselves and to know that, clichéd as it may sound, the truth will set us free.

There must be a middle way, tempered by the dictates of conscience, between the relentless scourge of a punishing guilt that can never be overcome and the egocentric pretense of a freedom and self-determination that know no bounds. To approach that way—a way of living honestly—we need to go back, back to the roots of the human need for confession. Where did this drive come from? How was it practiced and shaped in the generations before us? Why did it fall into disuse? And how can it help us now?

the ancient balm

The Origin of Confession

THE FIRST CONFESSION was not witnessed by any television camera, reporter, counselor, or priest. Let us imagine what took place, with little fanfare, at the dawn of civilization.

It is a few million years ago. In one corner of a cave, we have a man, woman, and child: the Us family. In the other, a man, woman and child: the Them family. It is quite a desirable cave for its time, offering protection from the elements and a narrow entrance so that a hungry saber-toothed tiger doesn't wander in, looking for easy prey. After all, the Us and Them families, hairy, two-legged creatures, can't run that fast, have pitifully small teeth and no claws, their only protection a sharpened stick or as big a rock as their puny frames can heft.

Us and Them have little contact, warily regarding each other as potential enemies, sharing nothing. That is the world they live in. They just happen to inhabit the same cave. They cannot speak; their powers of reasoning are barely a cut above animal instinct. They think—if we can call it that—much like children, in a series of imaginative pictures. They act impulsively, not systematically, in accordance with those pictures. Rational thinking would not play a part of the life of these, our forebears, for a tiny slice of time—the last twenty or thirty thousand years or so.

Father Them, being stronger than his mate (though Mother has gathered her share of berries, fruits, and nuts and killed a predator or two), does the hunting. He goes out early one morning and comes upon a young boar yelping away at the bottom of an arroyo, one leg broken by a fall. He promptly stones the unfortunate beast to death and drags the carcass back to the cave. After a good full meal of the raw flesh, the Them family falls asleep.

In the corner where the Us family is huddled together on a bed of dried leaves, the smell of fresh meat is more than they can stand. They haven't eaten for days. Father Us stealthily creeps over, tears off a leg, and creeps back to his family, who eagerly rip it to shreds. The crunching of a femur wakes Father Them. He looks down at his prize, at the spot where there was once a leg, and picks up a rock. His instincts tell him he has to protect himself and his own, and the only way that he knows to do that is to kill anything or anyone who threatens his survival.

He slowly makes his way to the other side of the cave, menacingly straightening up as tall as his chimpanzee-like body will allow. Mother Us and Baby Us watch him, terror in their eyes. Father Us trembles. They know what fate awaits them. Only the strong survive. And if the male is killed, the family will perish. Reasoning Father Us may not yet have, but he senses the law of cause and effect. Father Us picks up his own rock and rises to his full height.

But then Father Us does something never done before in the development of humankind, something that will set him apart from all who have gone before him. Flickering through the neurons of his still-evolving brain are a couple of fuzzy, ill-formed realizations: He is much bigger. I am going to die.

Father Them is glaring; his eyes meet those of Father Us. And instead of glaring defiantly back, Father Us lowers his gaze. His fingers loosen their grip; the rock falls to the floor of the cave with a resounding thud.

Father Them hisses and grunts with anger, stomping his bare feet on the ground, pounding his chest. He is ready to do battle—but to no avail. Father Us stands there, unwilling to defend himself for his action. He is, as we would say today, "owning it."

Something is happening. If we look closely, we can discern the dawning of a primitive emotion—nothing approaching "I've done something wrong." The ability to know right actions from wrong, the forming of a conscience, are yet many, many millennia away. Guilt? Hardly. Terror? For sure. But also Father Us's realization that he could either acknowledge what he'd done or face a battle to the death.

Dumbfounded by Father Us's tacit surrender, Father Them stares at his adversary. Father Us drops his shaggy shoulders still further. With a deep-throated grunt, Father Them wheels around and goes back to his side of the cave.

If we take a still closer look, we can tease out the basic elements of what we now know as confession. What we have witnessed shows little difference, in essence, from what occurs today in a therapist's or clergyman's office or before millions of television viewers. One human being did something wrong and with downturned eyes "admitted" his offense. With a grunt, Father Them acknowledged his acceptance.

Common sense, unformed as it was, had triumphed over retribution. Life in the cave could go back to normal.

From Taboo to Laws—
an Evolution

It is fascinating to speculate on the roots of confession. When, actually, did that first being—developing en route to what we consider fully human—truly understand that he or she had done something wrong, was willing to risk admitting it, and wanted to be released from the consequences?

No one knows, of course, but we do know that as human beings gathered in groups to better survive the harsh world around them, the need for some semblance of order arose. It meant that certain actions could no longer be tolerated. While the lone hunter-gatherer might kill anything that came across his path, within larger groups he could no longer do so.

Certain actions, such as incest, rape, stealing, and the desecration of sacred objects, became taboo because they disrupted the fragile network of relationships that helped to create a somewhat orderly way of living. The perpetrators of these forbidden acts either stopped and made retribution or faced expulsion or death. Primitive society was being ordered out of necessity, an animal instinct for survival. And as the loose rules that bound this society began to coalesce, they were internalized. The sense of danger that caused

Father Us to set down his rock became the unsettling hint of anxiety that followed infractions.

In their dreams, our ancestors were visited by women they had raped, children they had beaten, and fellow cave dwellers they had killed, along with a sheltering tree and animals that displayed great powers. The most memorable of these harsh storms of the mind and occasional comforting moments turned into legends and folktales, which were passed down orally from generation to generation. Gods in the likeness of animals were created to appease while other gods were believed to be intercessors, to make the rains come or stop, to produce a healthy child, to bring the herds of wild animals within reach. Primitive men and women, stirred by their anxieties, struggled to cope with the shouts and whispers received by their ever growing brains.

Slowly, taboos against unacceptable actions that haunted dreams and disrupted daily lives began to grow into codes, at first verbal, then eventually written. Because the codes contributed to a more stable society, they were accepted. And if the codes were defied, the group offended, the gods who ruled their fate (as people were certain they did) would have to be appeased. Retribution would be made, from a return of the spear or wife that had been taken to the death of an offender.

Throughout the ancient world—in disparate groups that could not have had contact with one another and without the influence of religious belief as we know it today—a new and common thread gently wove itself through the ongoing mystery of life on this planet: the development of consciousness. From the high civilizations of Egypt and Greece to scattered aboriginal tribes in the tropical Pacific basin and the frigid north of what is now Canada, the confessing of actions or even attitudes that would later be called sins—and the meting out of retribution or punishment for these wrongdoings—was taking hold.

THE EGYPTIAN SCALE

Beginning as early as 5000 B.C.E., one of the ancient world's first real civilizations flourished along the fertile banks of the Nile. For the Egyptians, the concept of Maat emerged as an ideal to guide the actions of diverse tribes with conflicting interests. Maat was not a system of written laws, such as the ones the Jews would begin to shape some 3,700 years later, but an overriding principle that embraced all aspects of life, from yearly celestial movements to daily social actions. The goddess Maat exemplified goodness; her image was venerated in temples as the personification of truth. Truth, the Egyptians had discovered, so underscored everything they did that it not only deserved worship, but obedience. Without truth, there was chaos. Without truth, no morality, no real justice, no order. Without truth, principles were not the limestone blocks of their pyramids, but little more than river silt to be washed away with the next rain.

The Egyptians understood themselves to be mortal beings, but beings containing the seed of the divine. Today we would call that seed the soul, and their Maat a religious framework. But the Egyptians didn't see a difference between the sacred and the earthly. All was sacred; all was earthly. And then there was a final reckoning. If your life was righteous and that divine seed nourished, you would gain eternal life. Awaiting you at death, in the Egyptian underworld, was the ultimate test: a scale. On one side of the balance bar was an upright feather, representing Maat. On the other, the deeds of your life. These were measured against a negative confession— sins not committed—the Forty-Two Declarations of Purity or, as it was known to the ancient Egyptians, *The Book of Going Forth by Day*. The Declarations' range was far more comprehensive than the mere Ten Commandments decreed thousands of years later. Some examples of the Declarations include:

I have not lied.

I have not taken milk from the mouth of children.

I have not caused pain.

I have not depleted the loaves of the gods.

I have not killed.

I have not ordered to kill.

It was an exacting performance evaluation, and Egyptians were taught from early childhood the standards demanded of them. They would ultimately face a sweeping confession that would determine whether they were spun back into life to try harder next time or waved on to their eternal reward.

Unspoken Codes

Thousands of miles to the west, and predating the rise of Egyptian civilization, the North American land mass emerged from the last ice age and the people we call the First Nations were beginning to inhabit its forbidding terrain. When modern-day anthropologists discovered the Saulteaux Indians in Manitoba, they found a society untouched by outsiders, an aboriginal people descended from the First Nations with no fear of God or gods nor of punishment by the state. Yet they had a highly developed sense of moral cause and effect.

Traditionally, the Saulteaux considered any illness or disease a punishment for what anthropologists interpreted as "bad conduct." And as any physical impairment could limit the ability to survive in this harsh environment, they were careful to avoid the offending conduct. If they stepped outside the social code of their tribe, anxiety was their warning signal. If a man lusted after his brother's wife, anxiety. If someone coveted a neighbor's fertile, level field, anxiety. If one hunter took a quick shot to beat out another just as he was ready to let his arrow fly, anxiety.

When anxiety became untenable, confession entered the picture. In order to keep or regain their health, offenders had to suffer the shame of self-exposure. It was believed that the medicine man could already see into the soul of the sinner, so there was little use in holding back. The exposure was not a quiet revelation but a public disclosure; the more grievous the crime, the more detail was needed to heap shame upon shame. But once the offense had been revealed to the Saulteaux community at large, it was considered washed away. As they put it, "bad conduct will not follow you anymore."

There were no formal rules or negative confessional edicts among the Saulteaux, yet children learned quickly what was expected of them. Anthropologists noted that "some feeling is gained of the kind of conduct that is disapproved." The public confessions in a crowded wigwam not only functioned to unburden the guilty; they were also morality plays that instructed and warned by example.

The Buddha's Way

The necessity of confessing wrongdoing turns out to be a common denominator among many religious traditions. Here, for example, from Maurice Walshe's *The Long Discourses of the Buddha* comes a wonderful story of what confession can and cannot effect.

King Ajatasattu, who in the fifth or fourth century B.C.E. ruled a huge swath of what is now northern India, came to the throne after brutally killing his mother and father. Later, his conscience gnawing at him, he decides to see a holy man—and not just any holy man, but the Buddha himself.

Penitent, the king leaves his retinue behind and goes on foot like any pilgrim to see the great man. Surrounded by his *bhikkhus,* or monks, the Buddha listens patiently and renders his judgment: "Since you have acknowledged the transgression and confessed as is right, we will accept it. For he who acknowledges his transgression and confesses it for betterment in the future, will grow in the noble discipline."

However, this is not the Buddha's last word. When the king has left, he says to the *bhikkhus,* "The king is done for;

his fate is sealed." He does not punish the king further and, in fact, allows him to leave feeling better. But he doesn't want his monks to believe that simply confessing such a horrendous deed is sufficient or that they will not suffer if, in the days ahead, they steal or cheat or kill to get what they think they desire.

It is an insightful application of confession, allowing the sinner to reduce the burden of sin but also keeping societal norms intact. And if we think about it for just a second, a perfect combination.

An Ancient Men's Group

Though cleansing and a release of guilt are the common threads of confessional practices across various time periods and belief systems, confession has also served as a sort of preventative medicine. When the Ku Waru warriors of Papua New Guinea were about to launch any risky activity that required close cooperation—like going into battle— they first took time to set themselves right. Not only overt actions, but even hidden feelings had to be revealed.

The Ku Waru men would go to a secluded spot in the jungle, kill and roast pigs, and as they shared the meal, confess to each other the items they had stolen and the animals they had mistreated. But there was still more on the agenda. The Ku Waru believed that feelings such as anger or jealousy would sap their strength and cause them to be wounded or even killed. Only through confession could these pent-up negative emotions be neutralized.

Is this not a precursor of the men's groups (and before them, women's groups) that began to emerge in the 1970s and '80s in developed countries? Something intrinsic to what it is to be human stirred inside the Ku Waru—and us. Only by facing our faults, misdeeds, and hateful or jealous thoughts could we be made whole again. Only then would they and we be at full strength and ready to face a marauding tribe . . . or the kids at home.

From the fourteenth to the early sixteenth centuries, Aztec high priests in what is now central Mexico went even a step further. They would not only hear confessions but would also, like military chaplains, go into combat with their warriors. If a warrior killed an innocent without cause, his sin could burden the entire force the next day and the next. A battlefield confession released them from their sin and prepared them to fight again, this time with honor and dignity.

Fast-forward to an Alcoholics Anonymous meeting today. "Hello, my name is _____, and I'm an alcoholic." Bill W., AA's prescient founder, saw that confession was the external and critical first step before any internal change could begin.

the birth of conscience

Jewish Thought, the Catholic Church, and the Protestant Reformation

A S A CHILD growing up in the early 1950s, I had only a shadowy knowledge of the presence of conscience in my own life. There was right and there was wrong. Each week in Catholic school, I dutifully, head hung low, entered the confessional booth and revealed how I had betrayed my God, hoping to avoid the fires of hell.

Who needed a conscience?

When I talked back to my mother, missed a prayer before a meal, pinched Nancy Bayer's arm or Kathy Brezina's more alluring areas as we ran around the St. Benedict's

School playground, I knew my reckoning was at hand. Catholic Confession was as regular as the weekly baths that we—all seven children in my family—took in a claw-foot bathtub. Free will, conscience—these were terms psychologists of the day might have used, but we did not. Each Saturday afternoon, we would enter the confessional booth to measure our lives by the Ten Commandments we could easily recite by heart.

Strangely, I treasure that experience. Rote as it could become, I was being called to a high standard. I failed miserably most of the time, but each week provided an opportunity to start again.

The rules I knew so well date back to around 1446 B.C.E., when Moses enshrined the Ten Commandments on two slabs of stone. Actually, the edicts would not have been that unfamiliar to him; they had their origin in the codes of conduct of other early civilizations.

The Code of Hammurabi, written in 1760 B.C.E. in pagan Babylonia, featured 282 laws meting out punishments ranging from straightforward cash payments to the cutting off of an ear to death. It is not the only ancient mandate, just the best known; discovered fragments indicate there were many more sets of rules from other groups, now lost to history. All the codes contained fundamental human wisdom, prohibitions against actions that would rend the social fabric and proscriptions to improve the still-evolving human being. But with the Ten Commandments, something in the equation changed dramatically. No longer would humans be second-guessing the gods, trying with their rituals to appease and please, to keep the gods' wrath at bay. Now there was a single point to which they addressed their concerns, a single beacon by which they steered their lives. "I will be your God and you shall be my people." (Exodus 6:7)

A simple and elegant promise, but as history would attest, not so simple for the chosen people to fulfill. Although the Ten Commandments pointed to a different kind of life, where not brute strength or tribal loyalty but justice would reign, there was still a tendency to revert to the old ways. Idol worship did not disappear. Golden calves were still cast and worshiped. Vestal virgins danced and were sacrificed.

This pact between God and that tiny, otherwise inconsequential tribe of Israelites did not deal so much in the threat of earthly punishments as in the verdict of eternal reward or damnation.

There was a certain internal integrity to this new way that was inspired and appealing. It was direct, offering mandates from God on how to live a worthwhile life before

Him, with accountability to Him alone. It resonated within the minds of ancient Jews: This was a better way to live, not only to please this God they were coming to know, but to make the world they inhabited more manageable. There was an implicit promise, borne out in the First Psalm: "For the Lord watches over the way of the righteous, but the way of the wicked will perish." Correct behavior—goodness, honesty, respect, self-control, purity—ultimately marked a more auspicious path.

Though the Jew was to examine his life through daily prayer, the yearly observance of Yom Kippur served as the Day of Atonement and Accounting. Commemorating Moses' bringing down the second tablet of commandments from Mount Sinai, the fast rounded off the period of ten High Holy Days that began with Rosh Hashanah, the start of the New Year and the day on which, according to Jewish tradition, God writes a person's fate for the *next* year into the Book of Life. On Yom Kippur the fate is sealed.

Ten days to decide. Will we continue as we have before? Or will we change, come closer to our beliefs, our adherence to the Ten Commandments, to our God?

In early Judaism, the temple high priest atoned for the sins of the people on Yom Kippur. In the Book of Numbers, the underpinning for the holy day, a sin offering was brought forth by the princes of the tribes of Israel in order to make amends with God—not so far removed from the offering of sacrifices to idols. But gradually Yom Kippur became more of a time for individual introspection.

During the rabbinical era, roughly C.E. 70–500, Yom Kippur was codified into a gathering at the synagogue in which people took stock of their lives, confessed their failings, and prayed. Sins were confessed and amends were made to assure God of one's sincerity. Fasting and abstaining from worldly pleasures disposed Jews to look deeply and clearly into their actions of the year past and the one dawning.

When the ancient temples were destroyed and the Jews dispersed, rabbinic ingenuity found a way to make observance at once more portable and more universal. One rabbi, upon finding the Second Temple in ruins, is said to have wailed to another rabbi that all was lost; there was now no possibility of atonement, of forgiveness. The Jewish people were doomed, unforgiven. "There is another atonement," his friend replied, "the doing of good deeds." Talmudic scholars would continue to stress a reading of the holy day in which the mere confessing of a sin was not enough and in fact did not bring forgiveness unless the sinning stopped and "righteous actions" replaced the flawed. Only then could you be forgiven.

From Rabbi Robert Waxman

WHY DO WE CONFESS?

Why do we confess? Because we have a desperate need for a clean slate from time to time.

Human beings have two sides, constantly in conflict. This side wants the easy way. The other side demands, or at least tends toward, righteousness. People want to feel they are good, know they are good. So Jewish law, Halacha, which means "the way" or "the path," provides guidance, lets you know when you are off the path.

For an observant Jew, there are prayers three times a day, set times for introspection, to improve yourself, which parallel monastic practice in the Christian tradition, wherein monks go to chapel and pray as many as six times a day.

But most Jews atone for their sins on Yom Kippur. In other traditions, most obviously the Catholic, people have an intermediary in the clergyman. In ours, people go directly to God, but Jews do not believe that God maintains some sort of heavenly database of our offenses. We believe that on this one day of the year, we can atone for our sins and renew our efforts to be better people. That is the appeal, the draw, of Yom Kippur: Now, I have a clean slate; I can go on with my life.

Most of our lives are not black and white; most of our lives are about good and better, not good and evil. It is all about degrees. I hope to move people toward better.

Yom Kippur, for both the ancient Jews and Jews today—even those who may not attend another synagogue service the rest of the year—is a powerful day of reckoning. It is a day that summons all, from the wandering tribes to the observant modern-day Jew to the self-professed "cultural" or "secular" Jew to pause, reflect, repent, and change.

CHRISTIANITY—A NEW PATH

Yom Kippur is not just another example of the universality of confession. Jesus, an observant Jew himself, knew well the practices of temple-era Judaism, and his New Testament teachings demonstrate both his unique messianic message and his own traditional religious formation.

The early Christians, persecuted but enflamed by a new way of life in which love superseded laws, developed their own method of moral accounting. This was a new concept of love, *agape;* it was boundless, mirroring God's great love for His created beings, the kind of love Jesus manifested, unrestricted, never vengeful, always seeking the neighbor's good. The six hundred and three mitzvot or commandments by which the Jews lived were superseded by just two: Love God and love your neighbor as yourself.

At first, there was a concern that if one violated the ethic of love and committed a horrible offense—murder, adultery, apostasy—there would be no chance of redemption. The early Christians eventually found a path to reconciliation: the public and communal admission of the instances in which they had strayed from "the Way" Christ had offered. Within their small communities, they would be given penances, ranging from restitution, with interest, of ill-gotten goods to the proclamation of their sins in the village square to self-flagellation.

The idea that a person could actually form a personal judgment on his or her actions was not yet part of the equation. The threat of banishment from the earthly religious community and of eternal damnation—especially in the first centuries after Christ, when the end-time was believed to be so near—regulated behavior very effectively. The concept of an internal mechanism, a conscience that could judge whether an action was bad and harmful or good and useful, began to emerge around the fourth century, with St. Augustine and his famous *Confessions.* A lusty pagan who converted to Christianity and became the bishop of Hippo, in North Africa, Augustine told about his early dissolute life and how unhappy it made him. Only when he publicly acknowledged his sins of whoring and gluttony and set out to live a new life in line with the moral code of his newly embraced Church did he find relief.

After Augustine, as the Roman Empire and its strict rule of civic conduct were crumbling, a group of ascetics known as the Desert Fathers left cities to find God in uninhabited wastelands. Seeking to live a life closer to God and to avoid the fires of hell, they would tell their elders of both their temptations and their failings.

Irish monks in the seventh century even drew up little guidebooks for confessors, called penitentials, telling them what to listen for and how to assist in the healing of souls. Specific sins equaled specific penances. Sins of the flesh could merit a year's diet of bread and water. A little thievery, plunging those itchy hands into freezing water over and over again.

But some clergy would also ask if the action was voluntary or involuntary, premeditated or an accident. A more personal approach to confession was beginning to take shape.

Confession as a Means of Control

Confession, it must be said, had enormous appeal. In fact, some historians point to the practice, even at its early stages of development prior to its institutionalization as a sacrament, as one of the reasons the Roman Catholic church grew so quickly. There was relief at unburdening one's soul of the anguish caused by wrongful acts. The guilty individual who entered a monk's cell to tell of his or her sins was a different person upon leaving.

Christianity would find confession useful not only as a means of cleansing and redirecting a soul, but also as a powerful tool of governance, which it used increasingly to maintain discipline and, beyond obedience, obeisance. At times the ardent beliefs of the faithful were subsumed by the legalistic organization the Church became. And as the Church grew in size and power, taking more of a role in regulating the lives of its followers—many of whom, like the general population, were illiterate—an easily understood set of standards of right and wrong was required. The simple Gospel mandate to "love one another" eventually morphed into scalpel-thin definitions of certain types of sin. In fact, Catholic confession is considered the primary means by which medieval society enforced moral order.

In the twelfth century, the Vatican's Third Lateran Council regularized practices and a concrete ritual for the admission of sins and the assurance of forgiveness came into being. Confession was declared a sacrament, and Christians were required to confess their sins at least once a year. And priests, God's representatives on earth, were given the power to grant forgiveness. Such clerical power—the ability of one human being to forgive or condemn another to the fires of hell—opened the way for abuses. The "penance" for committing a sin might require that a certain amount of money be paid to a member of the hierarchy. Indulgences that assured a heavenly passage were bought and sold. But it would be shortsighted to focus only on the abuses of confession. For the faithful, during confession, they were participants in a sacramental drama in God's presence; they made amends, were forgiven, and could go on with their lives.

To put this in some perspective, we need to remember that for fifteen centuries, there were no other religious voices in the West. From the time of Christ to the Reformation, historic eras would come and go, but in the Western world, the Roman Catholic church remained the one constant. Its monasteries, churches, and centralized, hierarchical structure formed the only stable environment for the development and spreading of a unified moral code. Until the sixteenth century, the Catholic church, more often for better but sometimes for worse, was the supreme arbiter of what constituted a righteous life—and what needed to be confessed.

THE PROTESTANTS BRANCH OFF

Martin Luther and John Calvin, the two leaders of what would eventually be called the Protestant Reformation, were to sweep aside the Catholic church's organization, obedience to the pope, and the miasma of indulgences and clerical privilege. Their belief, at once radical and traditional, did not doubt the message of Christ and his commandment of love, but quarreled with the method by which an earthly organization should administer it. For Luther, an Augustinian monk, this doubt manifested as an internal agony. Was he truly being absolved from his sins via prayer and confession? As he meditated on the words of Paul's Epistle to the Romans, his question was apocalyptically resolved:

"The just person lives by faith."

Luther never condemned the actual practice of Confession, just the church's institutional role in parceling out pardon; from priest to priest, abbot to abbot, parish to parish, the sinner could never be sure what the penance might be or if it would be granted. Pardon came from God, Luther believed, and the penitent soul could and should go directly to God for absolution. A dramatic fork in the Christian road had been reached.

As the various Protestant expressions branched out from the early fathers, Luther and Calvin, churches formed and reformed, and confession took on many different manifestations. For the Quakers, their agitated movements, supposedly a prelude to divine revelation, were also a sign of their contrition. Methodists, Presbyterians, and

Baptists all held confession as essential in the ascent to holiness, but theirs was a silent admission, often in the midst of a congregation or in the form of a unison prayer. The Protestant tradition taught that God forgave thus: "As far as the east is from the west, so far has He removed our transgressions from us" (Psalm 103:12).

FROM LAW TO CONSCIENCE

The nineteenth century begat the search for a deeper understanding of why people acted as they did, how underlying influences could alter our decisions and how our intent interacted with those influences—an understanding we take for granted today. Sigmund Freud's theories of unconscious human motivation and his "talking cure" (certainly a kind of confession) would crystallize this movement. All the major Western religious traditions— mainline Protestantism, Judaism, and the Catholic church—fought him and his approach, steadfastly maintaining that only their rules, not individual judgments, had true merit. The 1832 decree of Pope Gregory XVI, who pronounced it "false and absurd, or rather mad, that we must secure and guarantee to each one liberty of conscience" still held sway.

Try as they might, however, the established religions could not hold back the concept that each person had an innate sense of right and wrong and could exercise free will. Ironically, some of the earliest Christians had maintained that this was what made a person truly human.

In the 1960s, a time when venerable institutions became automatically suspect, Protestants and Jews took a fresh look at beliefs and practices that had been unquestionably followed. And the Catholic church, often considered the most inflexible of religions, stunned the world during the Second Vatican Council (1962–1965), when the gathered bishops declared that the primacy of conscience would be written into one of its documents. Conscience was the supreme arbiter of a person's actions, superseding any institution or code or law, the Church fathers now maintained. In *Gaudium et Spes,* the Pastoral Constitution on the Church in the Modern World, the Church acknowledged: "For man has in his heart a law written by God; to obey it is the very dignity of man; according to it he will be judged. Conscience is the most secret core and sanctuary of a man. There he is alone with God, Whose voice echoes in his depths."

In its Declaration on Religious Liberty, *Dignitatis Humanae,* the council went even further, boldly declaring, "It is through his conscience that man sees and recognizes the demands of the divine law. He is bound to follow this conscience faithfully in all his activity, so that he may come to God, who is his last end. Therefore he must not be forced to act contrary to his conscience. Nor must he be prevented from acting according to his conscience, especially in religious matters."

The caveman's animal, instinctual reaction had become a thinking person's considered choice. In a Church that had not markedly changed in centuries, many things had to give with this new approach. Though the sacrament of Confession still stood, it was dramatically affected. In 1965, as the Second Vatican Council was ending, nearly 40 percent of Catholics went to Confession monthly; today the number is 2 percent. And, even more telling, today 75 percent of Catholics say they either never go or do so less than once a year.

"Nothing like this had ever happened in the history of the Church," explained Father LaBaire. "Virtually overnight a sacrament that had been at the very heart of Catholic practice collapsed. Why? First, because people didn't like doing it. They were asked to recite a laundry list of offenses that didn't go into the why of those actions. There was a magical part to it: *Zap!* You are forgiven. Just sending somebody out with three Hail Marys as a penance was not going to do much to help them change behavior that was ruining their lives."

The strict moral codes of all the major faiths began to be looked upon as unduly legalistic, inflexible, and impractical in helping one navigate an increasingly complex world. A new term came into wider and wider use: situation ethics.

In a classic example, an attractive young woman is asked to spy on a factory that is polluting a city's water and killing infants. But the only way to gather the information she needs is to feign intimacy with the plant manager in order to gain his trust. What is she to do? Such promiscuity is against her beliefs. And yet a great good is at stake. An act that might otherwise be categorized as wrong might not be wrong in this case.

As thinking people shrugged off firm rules and stepped over boundaries that no longer held, the honest confession of wrongdoing, once a straightforward statement of frailty and a request for forgiveness, began its slow slide into disuse.

THERAPY—THE NEW CONFESSION

Meanwhile, the golden age of therapy was at hand. Therapy would become the way, the truth, and the life of many people who had once turned to religion for guidance. The approaches were clearly at odds with one another: Were the real answers within, graspable through self-reflection, or without, uniformly mandated by religious authority?

Freud—whose deep influence on nearly every strand of psychological discourse cannot be overstated—maintained that there were many elements outside humans' control that caused them to act as they did. And if those actions were aberrant or harmful, either to the person or to others, it was not as important to judge the action and punish the person as it was to free him from whatever it was that caused him to act that way. Each person was the sum of early admonishments received from parents or authority figures, healthy or unhealthy childhood and adolescent experiences, hereditary traits, and physiological development. Therefore, human acts must always be viewed in context. The same action by two people was not the same action at all.

Christianity's teaching was more absolute: Although all human beings are given free will to choose what is good and avoid what is evil, the choices are clear and the circumstances largely irrelevant. In Judaism, the Torah likewise provides a strict code of right and wrong.

While religious authorities resisted the notion of subliminal forces controlling human actions, and Freud and company railed against the mailed fist of eternal damnation wielded by those religious authorities, the demarcations between the two conflicting camps blurred in interesting ways over time.

Mainstream religions slowly began to understand—
and then teach—conscience as not merely a shifting fog to
hide the wily sinner, but as a divinely inspired and brilliant
light to guide a truly moral life. Rather than be held to an
absolute standard, individuals were continually required
to make judgments on their actions. Circumstances did
matter, but moral theologians would grant that argument
only so much credence. Regardless of a mother who weaned
them too early, a punitive father who withheld approval, or
any of the deep-seated shaping influences identified by the
psychoanalytic community, ultimately the individual would
have to accept responsibility for his actions. An "informed"
conscience was the goal, one that could make sound
judgments, even within a culture where shades of gray were
clouding what was once considered black and white.

Certainly we can see some synergy between Freud's
approach to human wholeness and that of the religions
he abhorred; we can easily view priest as therapist and
therapist as priest. Each is at the service of humankind, but
in different ways.

"In Freud's nonjudgmental approach toward his
own confessions, we can discern the move away from
religious toward humanitarian ideas. From this perspective,
confessions were no longer executed to obtain forgiveness;

instead they became a vehicle for insight and understanding into the universality of human foibles," writes psychologist Sharon Hymer in *Confessions in Psychotherapy.*

Psychoanalysis seeks to unearth the disorder caused by layers of repression. Confession seeks another truth—the truth of our inherent worth and goodness, our basic purity of soul, which has been not so much repressed as wasted, compromised, rationalized away with what we might call sin—acts and attitudes that are out of keeping with what is best in us.

There are many definitions of sin, but for our purposes, let us call a sin any act we knowingly do (or refuse to do) that injures or depletes ourselves or another person. It is a deliberate violation of a moral or religious law. It is a violation of our selves.

How do we know when we sin? It comes back to that mysterious force called conscience. "It is the saints who have a sense of sin," wrote the eminent twentieth-century French theologian Jean Danielou. "The sense of sin is the measure of the soul's awareness of God."

A Gentler Concept of God

At mid-twentieth century, Swiss physician Paul Tournier applauded the movement away from absolutist standards

From Rabbi Robert Waxman

"SIN"

K arl Menninger's book *Whatever Became of Sin?* aptly summarizes what is at the root of our present dilemma: We have a need to realign ourselves with that higher self within, yet we have a reluctance to do so and a lack of knowledge about exactly how.

We don't like to use the word *sin* anymore. The typical attitude is, "What you may think is sin is my normal lifestyle. How dare God tell us what to do?"

Yet people have this self-loathing; they know when they have offended.

It is tragic to be able to diagnose the illness and not be able to apply the treatment.

of behavior. Like many of his colleagues, he was heavily influenced by Freud. But as he became more deeply involved in his counseling practice, he came to feel that something had been lost in the total acceptance of therapy as a substitute for the balm of religious ritual. The talking cure dealt with mental and emotional suffering yet gave no credence to spirit. As Tournier's contemporary, the philosopher Paul Ricoeur, so eloquently put it, "What a wilderness it is, or rather a castle of Kafka, when . . . man has lost the sense of forgiveness while retaining his sense of sin."

Tournier could not, he felt, simply prescribe a sedative and send his patients on their way, yet the hyperpunitive Calvinistic beliefs of his upbringing were unlikely to bring solace. He looked to Freud's conclusion that guilt is aroused in children out of the fear of loss of parental love and concluded that, by extension, hellfire-and-brimstone sermons and admonishments and penances would only serve to exacerbate his patients' suffering. "At the heart of personality is the need to feel a sense of being lovable without having to qualify for that acceptance," Tournier wrote in his seminal book, *Guilt and Grace.* Moreover, he wrote, "Nothing makes us so lonely as our secrets."

So he argued for and began to incorporate into his work a gentler conception of God, one whose acceptance could loosen guilt's stranglehold and let his patients breathe in the fresh air of forgiveness. God was not angry at the foibles of woman and man, Tournier assured his readers, but readily embraced each of us in our totality.

The God Tournier offered to his patients is the God that makes sense to me personally. I believe this God can offer comfort to anyone, with or without formal religious beliefs. I am not a theologian, but I question the idea that God would create us, give us free will, and then punish us on a daily basis for our mistakes. Why, like any reasonably good parent, should God not be forgiving and welcoming, full of unconditional love?

Each Thursday, I visit Catholic patients at a local hospital, taking them Holy Communion. On a cold January day in the Carolinas, I came into Jane's room. Her hair, patchy and unruly, a swirl of different colors and textures, had grown back after the first round of chemotherapy, and only a lone saline solution bag hung on the IV pole beside her bed, so it was not immediately evident how she was doing. As we talked, it soon became clear: colon cancer, stage four. Further treatment would be suspended. And so, when I offered to give her Holy Communion and she looked down, murmuring that she could not receive it, I asked why.

"It was a Catholic school in England," she began in a quiet voice, with only the slightest tinge of a British accent. "On Mondays, sister would ask those of us who hadn't been to Mass on Sunday to raise our hands. I was only six years old; lying wasn't in my nature. So, I raised my hand. Those of us who had raised our hands were ushered outside the room to be caned. Across our backs and backsides. I came back into the room, trying so hard not to cry, but it hurt. Inside and out.

"I did that a few more times and was caned each time. Then it dawned on me what to do when the Monday morning question was asked. I kept my hand down; I lied.

"That was my first impression of the Church, of God punishing me because my parents hadn't taken me to Mass, that I was bad. In fact, I *deserved* to be beaten with that cane."

Jane knew only punishment and guilt for her "sin," if you want to call it that. She experienced none of God's mercy for us frail and fragile humans. Although Jane was a woman of faith, somehow she didn't see that there was nothing that could alienate her from her maker or from the basic goodness that she obviously possessed.

As for me, I cannot hope to face myself, in a confessional booth or in the quiet solace of my nightly reflections, without the confidence that I do not wage my battles alone. I have known strict religious rules; I have been psychoanalyzed. The rules have changed; the earth has shaken. But there is that Something beyond my consciousness, unknowable, mysterious, that will not abandon me.

CHAPTER FOUR

seeking realignment

Following One's Inner Compass

N THIS MAGNIFICENT and sometimes confusing symphony that plays within each of us, there are so many notes and chords—experience, genes, upbringing, culture, and psychological makeup among them—some coming together beautifully, others with deafening, self-destructive dissonance. Daily, consciously and unconsciously, we seek to blend, shape, or alter these elements in our own unique way. I don't think I am alone in making promises to myself: Today, yes, today, I will do better. I won't make the same mistakes. I will seek light, not darkness. I want to be the person I know I truly am.

We are seeking realignment.

Moral or spiritual consciousness is also shaped from our earliest influences and the choices we made growing into mature adults. But if we pause for a moment to reflect back on how we have lived our lives—and how happy or unhappy we have been with our actions—most of us recognize that there has always been that quiet voice in the background of the din or silence of our days. Our conscience.

Marc D. Hauser, a Harvard professor of psychology and human behavior, studied the biological roots of moral judgments and conscience by presenting complex moral dilemmas that had no easy answer: Would you drive your boat faster to save the lives of five drowning people knowing that a person in your boat will fall off and drown? Would you give a drug to a person to better preserve their organs for transplant even though the drug will make them die sooner? He found that people with remarkably different backgrounds answered very much the same. From believers and atheists, rich and poor, educated and not, the answers were similar. What was equally remarkable was that when asked why they decided as they did, most *had no idea whatsoever.*

We don't need a learned psychologist or a survey or Jiminy Cricket to tell us what we already instinctively know: The true home of our conscience is not within our limited rational powers. Its true home is beyond reason. I believe it is a part of us untouched by anything other than the divine, our soul. Even among those who do not share this belief, it is rare to find anyone arguing the position that they are deaf to a quiet voice within—whatever they care to call it. We all grapple with its urgings, sometimes heeding them, sometimes refusing to hear.

The Inner Compass

In my Navy days, peering out at a black, starless sea from the bridge of my ship, I would continually look down at the compass by which I steered the course. It was a simple enough device, but a powerful one: a needle lined up with the natural magnetic field of our earth.

So, too, each of us has an inner compass that tells us when we are on or off course. The initial pleasure we felt stealing that candy from a supermarket shelf in grade school was inevitably followed by a sense of unease—our conscience at work. Cheating in business to get ahead; betraying a friend; violating a trust; turning one's back on a brother, sister, mother, or father; eating more than is healthy; abusing alcohol, other drugs, or sex could all disturb our internal magnetic field.

Thomas Hood called conscience "that fierce thing," and Hamlet had to admit that "conscience does make cowards of us all." For most of us, it doesn't have to be that poetic. As simple as it sounds, when we betray our conscience, it just doesn't feel right.

More often than not, our wrongdoings aren't a dramatic departure. They are incremental choices, shifting that needle not from 0 to 180, but a half degree here and a couple of degrees there. Think about the story of the very successful Texas basketball coach, Dave Bliss, who was forced to resign after one of his players killed a teammate. The investigation showed that Bliss's contribution to a poisonous environment had started with little lies, like faking a star player's grades to keep him on the team or not reporting failed drug tests, and eventually mushroomed into tens of thousands of dollars in illegal payments to players, one of whom was the murderer. The schools for which he coached were delighted with his winning teams, and Bliss went from lie to lie to succeed, drifting further and further off course, shifting just a small degree at a time.

The inner compass, our conscience, can only tell a true course. Try as we might to bend that compass needle to our will, to a course it is telling us not to follow, we cannot. It is through the honesty of confession that we are able to stop and reset our course.

GUILT IN PERSPECTIVE

Many of us have a dark corner where a secret lurks, a secret that has power over us, that we will do anything to avoid looking at squarely. It has far more power, we rationalize, than we could ever deal with. Why fight the unfightable? So we give in.

The therapeutic world calls them defense mechanisms, unconscious reactions we have to uncomfortable circumstances or behaviors. For instance, an alcoholic may counter criticism by saying how well he or she functions at work. Defense mechanisms allow us to keep the illusion of self-esteem. Or, that we are indeed "on course." If we do not confront our demons, we can convince ourselves that we are in control here and that our failings do not need to be confronted, are minor, or are someone else's problem. There is a sweet seduction that goes on in our minds wherein we fashion ourselves as dominant. Actually we are being dominated.

The hitch is that as we desperately try to avoid introspection, performing all sorts of contortions to shield our secrets from the outside world, they become even more powerful. When we lie to ourselves, we necessarily develop a split personality: the liar and the one who knows the truth. "Secrets that remain hidden grow in importance or bizarreness, having never had the chance to be tested in the interpersonal realm," writes Sharon Hymer in *Confessions in Psychotherapy,* getting at the heart of the efficacy of confession in forcing our darkest parts into the light.

Is it so surprising that guilt, more than any other emotion, keeps people from facing themselves, from airing out these secrets? The guilty believe they have done something so wrong, lived so rottenly, squandered so absolutely that there is no hope for them. They may feel outside that circle of concern, beyond the reach of divine love, even beyond the love of family and friends. The compass is hopelessly beyond repair. They wear not an *A,* the scarlet letter of an adulterer or adulteress, but the *G* of the permanently guilty.

Coming from a time and place where guilt was a staple, I can empathize with those who trudge through life with a burden they can neither carry nor throw off. As I have dealt with this in my own life—my guilt over failures as a single and married man, as a son and a father—I have come to view guilt in another way. Guilt is like basil, the herb. A little sprinkled on top of a dish is useful, but you can't make a meal out of basil—or make a life out of guilt. Unfettered guilt is debilitating. Its by-product, anxiety, can gnaw away at a person's core, perpetuating a cycle wherein even a hint of a fault produces a seismic reaction. The guilty person is always under suspicion, always on trial. True, it is an internal, self-inflicted indictment, but it is painful nonetheless.

From Sister Karen Kirby

FRIENDS WITH QUICK ANSWERS

n the Well Spring Catholic Bookstore, as we stand off to the side and leave books behind and dive headlong into life, I often hear that a person in trouble has tried to talk to a well-meaning friend, but it didn't work. The friend wasn't really listening. The friend gave some snap solution.

That is the beauty of the bookstore. It is a leisurely place. A holy place, really. It is a place where people come because they want to know more.

I pray with them and my prayer is quite simple: Don't try to face this alone. The God that is aware of every feather that falls to the ground from every bird is aware of you. Let God help you. Let him mend your broken heart. Let him help you find a new path in life. Let him release you from your guilt. You are not alone.

And yet a certain amount of guilt can be very useful.

Guilt can be the beginning of the cure, a way to overcome the power of our secrets, a stimulus for change.

Honest guilt can instill what analysts and spiritual counselors call the anxiety of responsibility. It can prompt us to take responsibility for our actions. This happens not only in a therapist's office or confessional booth. It can happen over a cup of coffee with a friend, in the quiet of our bedrooms, or as we peer out the window of an airplane. It happens when we put pretenses and defenses aside and decide to tell the truth to and for ourselves.

AGAINST SELF-PUNISHMENT

As a child, saying my nightly prayers before my mother, I would always choose to kneel on a furnace grate, so that I could suffer for the sinful deeds of that day. As I piously mouthed the prayers I knew by heart, I was making a sort of internal confession, my mind racing over the times I spoke back to my parents, cheated on a test, or sneaked a peek at the girlie magazines my older brothers tucked under their mattresses. I was a wretched sinner, inflicting my own penance. In our religious traditions, we may have heard that our bread and our beard must be soaked in our tears for our many offenses. To atone for their sins, some penitents go on pilgrimages, where they inch along on their knees, wailing and crying to heaven. My choice was the furnace grate.

Self-punishment, practiced by Christians and non-Christians alike, has a long and lurid history. Flagellation came into popular use just before the dawn of the Middle Ages as plagues and epidemics swept through Europe; it was meant to placate God so he would deliver his people from these horrors. Whips of leather thongs, some studded with pieces of glass or metal, would turn a man's back into a bloody pulp. Ironically, the Brotherhood of the Flagellants, as they were called, probably helped spread the Black Death they hoped their suffering would alleviate.

Misguided penance, self-inflicted suffering, or over-scrupulosity perpetuates and accentuates what it is trying to erase. Wallowing in guilt paralyzes us, freezing in our minds an image of ourselves as beyond redemption. An overly scrupulous person performs excruciating examinations of conscience, recounting his "sins" over and over, sometimes even keeping a notebook of his faults.

And when the scrupulous person comes face-to-face with a failing, the tendency is to overcorrect, to go directly to what we see as the root of our problem and rigorously and perhaps obsessively recast our lives. If we have stolen, we "confess" to the supermarket manager that we took two plastic bags instead of one for our broccoli. If we doubt God, we spend hours in church or in prayer. If we feel we have not spent enough time with our children, we become the überparent, newly attuned to every need or even vague request from our children.

On the surface, it may look like a brave and honest approach, but scrupulosity is nothing if not self-hate, robbing a person of the normal resiliency and spontaneity that comes with an honest confrontation of both minor and major sins. It would seem to confront reality, but it escapes reality by imposing stern rules and requirements in the place of sensible, human, situation-specific judgments.

ASSESSING RESPONSIBILITY

Decisions, actions, events—millions of them—chart the path our lives will take. Most are what ethicists would call morally neutral, for instance choosing what car to buy, music to enjoy, socks to wear. But certain moments confront us with choices that steer us onto the high road or the low.

We are responsible when we make a conscious decision to do something we know to be wrong—whether it be a moral, spiritual, psychological, or legal violation. We must intend to do wrong, although few reasonably sane people would say, "I want to do something awful right now." Rather, we fool ourselves into the belief that what we are doing is perfectly all right, as we selfishly seek our own gratification

From Father Steven LaBaire

TELLING THE STORY

The chaos in people's lives also comes in lighter shades. These are the actions or habits we want to confess because they hold us back from living a full life. We sense there is a better way. A better way than screaming at our children every time they do something wrong. A better way than being impatient with an aging parent. A better way than talking behind people's backs, gossiping so much that people are hurt.

Whether the chaos be light or dark, people need to tell their story because they feel disconnected, isolated, alone. We are social beings; we yearn to be known and understood. Not to be known is to live in a certain hell. That is the benefit of telling the story, of confessing; it reconnects us with the rest of the human race. We discover that our chaos is not so unique or aberrant.

I see it time and time again in my practice, the way a face relaxes when I say something as simple as "You'll learn from that and you will do better next time; I just know it" or "This doesn't make you a bad person; it's just a misstep. Let it go and be open to the next chance to make a change. I know you can do it."

and trample the needs of others. Whatever the situation, we have gone against our best instincts and the voice of our conscience.

This discussion of responsibility is crucial to our understanding of the "what" of confession, because the line between real guilt and undeserved guilt is a fine one, difficult for us to see and even more difficult to act upon.

I offer an example from my own life, a very sad and painful occurrence. I was seventeen, a new driver, driving my mother to a hospital appointment. In trying to pass a slow-moving car in front of me, I lost control and was hit head-on by a pickup truck. My mother was killed.

I am often asked how that affected my life. This was a horrible accident; it took my mother's life. I went through many months of introspection and, looking back on my poor performance during the next few years in college, depression. Under layers of guilt, I felt the need to confess, but I didn't know what I would confess. Or how I could possibly make restitution. Eventually, I came to an uneasy peace with this chapter in my life. I was an impatient young man, inexperienced as a driver, but never did I will or want this to happen. I could mourn her death—I did, and I do— but I realized my mother would not want me to go through life with a burden of guilt for something unintentional. And if there was any restitution to be made, it would be that I would lead a worthwhile life; any mother would hope so for her son.

A State of Humble Self-Recognition

Most of the choices we make—to act in keeping with our moral compass or not, to make measured changes or resort to an OCD fixation—usually are made in circumstances where we are not threatened or coerced. In an atmosphere of freedom, which is the air most of us breathe, we have a certain luxury in the exercise of free will. But what if that very air is poisoned?

Viktor Frankl, a distinguished Austrian psychiatrist, survived three years in Nazi concentration camps. Night after night, desolate and depressed, he sat on the edge of his rough wooden bunk, having just experienced another day of man's cruelty to man. He was hungry and cold. His wife, parents, and brother had died in the camps. He knew he might not live another day; his life could be snuffed out by merely the wrong look in the direction of the wrong guard. He had no dignity, no possessions; he had lost everything. A man of letters, he knew well Dante's inscription on the entrance to hell in *The Divine Comedy*: ABANDON ALL HOPE YE WHO ENTER HERE. Many of those around him had.

How could he even think about morality in such an immoral place? How could he consult his moral compass when the world was so out of alignment? Everything had been stripped from him but one thing, he realized. His attitude. He could give in to the horrors of the camp, or hope for a better day. He could see each day as a living hell, or another day that he was still alive. He could give up or go on.

Frankl never professed strong religious convictions. If his credo would be written, it would be short, a single word: yes. Yes to life. Yes to possibility. Yes to going on. Yes to a belief that each life has meaning.

His is a powerful message as we explore our lives. Our state of mind is something we can control. We may have had traumatic experiences; we may be living in a horrible situation right now; we may feel weighed down by the burdens of our failings, mistakes, inadequacies. Guilt may wash over us, threatening to swallow even our best intentions. But any or all of these circumstances need not be the final word.

With Frankl's simple word on our lips, perhaps not even spoken, we can live its promise. We can look at ourselves with what I will call humble realism. We can see ourselves as a combination of so many good traits and possibilities but also home to some parts of us that make us sad or weary or wary of life. We can laugh at our stupidities, our failing again and again—at the very same thing, in the very same way!

Standing aside from ourselves, do we not at least faintly admire this person for having faced up to so many struggles? Does this life not have meaning? Are there not roads yet to be traveled, people to meet, experiences to be had, all with the humble realization that mistakes will be made, hurt will be felt and inflicted, but that this yes is the most sweeping, profound—and sometimes seemingly impossible—response to a chaotic world?

The other option is to say no. I will not believe in myself. I will not be humble; I will arrogantly shield myself from life. I will not be willing to believe that a simple yes is often the best I can do, all I can do, knowing that the yes will never mean that my life will be without its failures, knowing only that each failure or difficulty will present the choice over and over again, to which my yes is needed, each time, each day, as it was for Viktor Frankl.

My yes will produce some wonderful moments and possibilities, and I will be happy to have had them. I will also go off course and stumble and fall. I will sin again, and I will need to confess to myself and, at times, to others. I will need a deliberate pause in the anxiety of my life to humbly reflect on who I am, what I have done, who I want to be. But in that humble recognition, something will happen, so subtle that I will know it only when I look back on who I was once. I will have become a human being, a whole human being, the sum of parts favorable and unfavorable, admirable and detestable.

I will have begun to practice the art of living honestly.

praying backward through the day

And Other Helpful Techniques to Practice Living Honestly

"DREAMS ARE A bridge between our ego and our soul, or between our waking self and our deepest self. If this relationship is weak or lacking altogether, then we are in a state that psychologists refer to as unconsciousness, a state that is natural for animals and infants but far from desirable in adults. Our capacity for self-reflection is a measure of our spiritual development and psychological maturity, as well as a good predictor of the quality of our relationships." In this excerpt from *The Discerning Heart,* a book about perceiving one's spiritual path in life, Wilkie and Noreen Au discuss the value of analyzing the content of our dreams. I hope they will not mind if their words are applied to another form of introspection, that of daily examining our actions.

How is it possible for people to look deeply within—alone, regularly, and without professional help—to discover those faults, habits, and attitudes that are corrosive to their inner being, as well as detrimental in their daily life? Many of us do not know where to begin.

In this chapter, I offer some time-tested approaches and techniques that anyone can use to take that deeper look. Initially, they are much like a brace for a broken or misshapen bone, providing support as the bone itself seeks health and the correct disposition. Eventually, they become a natural and organic part of who we are.

Some of us use confession rituals within our religious traditions. But there are other ways, outside of formal religious services and rituals, some of which I present here. I hope one of these pathways—or your own combination—will provide a structure that resonates with you, a routine that you actually look forward to practicing. Please don't look upon the discipline of personal reflection—and confession—as one more thing you have to cram into an already overscheduled life. It is meant to lift burdens, not create them. Rather than a hand-wringing exercise, self-reflection asks for humility and simplicity, the ability to look clear-eyed and straightforwardly at ourselves and our actions as best as we can, within our own limitations.

Once we have decided to put aside our posturing and our masks, we may eventually find that this discipline is actually freedom—the freedom to know and choose relationships and actions that spring from the best part of us, that respond to the inner voice that murmurs, ever so softly, "Yes, this is me. This is good. Go on."

What may be effective for one person may not work for another. The voluble extrovert and the pensive contemplator experience life in different ways; they are "wired" differently. The objective is to make room for differences and not to apply one technique dogmatically.

Visit or Revisit Your Faith Tradition

As I drove up the winding road in Dharmsala, India, I couldn't help but notice the hundreds of people lining the road. Some were squatting, others sat lotus-style, and a small number were standing. Regardless of their position, most of them had their eyes closed in deep meditation. I turned to the interpreter who was taking me to my interview with the Dalai Lama. I didn't have to ask.

"They are the seekers. They have come to His Holiness from the four corners of the globe. They have come for enlightenment, to bask in his presence, just to be close to him. They hope to hear a word from him that explains the secrets of life, the secret of their life and what they are to do with it. Some have been here for years, eating whatever is given to them, sleeping wherever they can. They have no other desires."

The Dalai Lama is not a man who tries to hide his emotions, and a pensive—and compassionate—smile covered his face when I mentioned these pilgrims. "I am honored they have come to be with me, very honored. But I am afraid I do not have any answers at all. None. If they ask me for my advice, I must admit quickly I do not have the secret of life. I am a man, that is all. I do not tell them to become Buddhists and sit for hours in meditation. 'I am happy you have come,' I tell them, 'but now I must send you away. All good paths lead to God. Go back to your own faith tradition, go deeply into it. There you will find Him and you will find yourself.'"

As a first step, I would recommend listening to the Dalai Lama's wisdom: If you have one, go back to the religious tradition in which you were raised. Search it for the truths it holds and assistance it promises. You need not wait for the High Holy Days or Ramadan or Easter; go to the prayers of these holy occasions and enter into them with an open heart.

Our faith traditions have special days or seasons dedicated to self-reflection and confession. For Jews, it is Yom Kippur. For Christians, the penitential seasons of Lent and Easter. For Muslims, the fasting and introspection of Ramadan.

Looking at the words used at these times of self-accounting, we find striking similarities. We hear not only the voice of the divine, but the echoes of our response as flawed but hopeful human beings. We are imperfect beings. We make mistakes, admit them, ask for forgiveness, and try to live differently in the future.

For Jews, these are the words of Yom Kippur Shaharit:

You search the chambers of our inner being,
You examine the conscience and the heart.
There is nothing hidden from you,
Nothing is concealed before your eyes.
So let it be your will,
Eternal one, our God, God of our ancestors,
That you may grant forgiveness to us for all of our sins,
And be merciful to us for all of our injustices,
And let us atone for all we have done wrong.

For Lutherans, a prayer of confession:

> O Almighty God, merciful Father, I, a poor, miserable sinner, confess to You all my sins and iniquities, with which I have ever offended You and justly deserved Your punishment now and forever. But I am heartily sorry for them and sincerely repent of them, and I pray You of Your boundless mercy and for the sake of the holy, innocent, bitter sufferings and death of Your beloved son, Jesus Christ, to be gracious and merciful to me, a poor sinful being.

For Muslims, a recitation from the Hadith Qudsi:

> O son of Adam, so long as you call upon Me, and ask of Me, I shall forgive you for what you have done, and I shall not mind. O son of Adam, were your sins to reach the clouds of the sky and were you then to ask forgiveness of Me, I would forgive you. O son of Adam, were you to come to Me with sins nearly as great as the earth, and were you then to face Me, ascribing no partner to Me, I would bring you forgiveness nearly as great as it.

For Catholics, during the Sacrament of Reconciliation:

> O my God, I am heartily sorry for having offended Thee, and I detest all my sins, because I dread the loss of Heaven, and the pains of Hell; but most of all because I have offended Thee, my God, Who art all good and deserving of all my love. I firmly resolve, with the help of Thy grace, to confess my sins, to do penance, and to amend my life.

Seven Suggested Practices for Self-Reflection

Some of the self-reflective approaches below are broad and general, because often we do not know exactly where the problem lies. It may be hidden deep beneath the surface of our actions. For example, our intemperate rages without provocation may have nothing to do with the traffic jam, spouse, or child before us but everything to do with our underlying lack of self-worth or our nagging guilt. Other approaches are more specific—a list of prompts to ponder, to see where we are failing others and ourselves.

Let's begin with a classic method.

I. Observe, Judge, Act

This simple method was developed prior to World War II by a Catholic group seeking to translate the Church's teachings into concrete practice. It can be used on a daily basis or can be applied to individual moments, judgments, or feelings when we are confused by what faces us and want to change the way we habitually respond. The three steps of observing, judging, and acting embrace looking inward and acting outward.

You know that feeling of unease when something isn't right. I'm not right. I feel off balance. Well, pause and observe what's going on.

Observe: Be Specific About Something You Want to Change

You are a person easily irritated when people don't perform as expected. Beyond irritation, you find yourself flying into an uncontrollable rage too many times throughout the day. A clerk who doesn't know where to find the item you are looking for, a broken handle on a gas pump, a wide array of supposed infractions by spouse, children, or coworkers are all fertile ground for your anger. Your wife, your children, even some of your coworkers have mentioned your short fuse and lack of patience. Just to say "I must stop getting angry" isn't going to help much. Rather than working on your generic anger, take one example in your life, like your recent outburst at the new young trainee in your department. When he couldn't find a report you needed for a meeting, you had screamed: "Find it, damn it; do I have to do everything here!"

Judge: Consider the Consequences of Your Action

You walked into the meeting without the report, still steaming, and said to the team, "This kid has got to go; he can't do anything right." The young man had been there a week; this was not going to bode well for his future. Consider the other consequences: Now you have a trainee whose confidence is shattered and will live in fear of you, and colleagues who are taken aback by your outburst and perhaps wonder about your competence as a manager. But if you don't say or do anything, no one will know the circumstances. (In fact, when you really look into it, you had misfiled the report.)

Act: Do Something to Rectify the Situation

If you allow yourself to continue to vent your rage without thinking, you are never going to change. Now is the time to act. A simple apology to the trainee will go a long way. Look for an opportunity to help the trainee; walk through the steps you know by heart, but are still a mystery to him. And the next time he does something well, congratulate him and let the team members know about it. (One act breeds others: Hopefully you will find yourself stopping to think before you act out your anger in other situations as well.) And, at the next meeting, if you want to "confess" to your outburst (and misfiling of the report), you can, but otherwise show yourself to be someone who understands and accepts that mistakes will be made—especially by you.

2. Consolations and Desolations

Ignatius Loyola, the founder of the Jesuit order, was quite the sinner as a young man. A soldier and a playboy, he seemed to be following a well-trod path for men of his day in sixteenth-century Italy, until he was injured in battle and forced into a long period of recuperation. Instead of the popular books of adventure, he began to read the biographies of saintly men and women. Something stirred within him. He found himself not only interested, but excited about their lives. The sour aftertaste of his dissolute life and interests faded, replaced by a longing to live heroically another way, in service to others.

Ignatius would eventually become one of history's great spiritual masters, and his thirty-day Ignatian retreats are still enormously popular. Every Jesuit is required to take at least one monthlong retreat; lay women and men have also found them life-changing. Part of the discipline that Ignatius recommended was a very simple technique: consolations and desolations. He asked his followers to spend a few moments each night recalling the moments in which they felt most alive and worthwhile that day and those in which they felt the opposite, dead inside and worthless.

Ignatius did not have the benefit of modern psychoanalytic theory, but it was his experience that God did indeed speak through our deepest feelings and yearnings and that we should listen to them.

You may find it useful to set aside a specific time and place to consider the consolations and desolations of the day, beside your bed, in a favorite chair, or even standing in the darkness of a room. Allow your mind to wander through the day that is ending. Here are a few prompts:

What did I do that made me happiest?
Where did I feel ashamed of myself?
Did I act selfishly or for the good of others?
What action would I do over again and how?
What moved me to act the way I did?
What habits or tendencies worked for or against me?
When did I feel most in alignment with what is best in me?

Stay with the feeling and allow it to lead you inward. Consider how you may want to avoid or change the circumstances or attitude that caused desolation. See if you can put yourself in a position to experience more consolation.

3. Praying Backward Through the Day

Mystics and tortured souls, from those whose inner life was vibrant to those whose very existence was in shambles, have instinctively utilized a simple process I call praying backward through the day.

I could easily have called it thinking through the day or reflecting about the day. I purposely use the word *praying* because I believe that too many of us rely only on our tiny brains and thimbleful of knowledge as we try to confront who we are and what we could be.

I have a rather simple concept of God, a theology with a foundation in a few years of formal education but more informed by years of life experience. I do not pretend to understand our Creator's ways, who He (or She) is, or why things happen as they do. But as a creator myself (a parent) and the product of creation (by my parents), I know that creators only want what is best for those they have brought into being. Even though we may not know it at the time, our eternal parent loves us and is there to help as we stumble, fall, mature, lapse, and struggle to grow. God or a higher power is involved in our lives—no, not by direct commands, but through a gentle urging that we might see ourselves as He sees us. And that we might act accordingly.

Here's an apt description from an unlikely mystical writer, F. Scott Fitzgerald. In *The Great Gatsby* young Nick Carraway assesses the way the fabulous Gatsby regards him: with "an incredible prejudice in my favor." Could or would God do less?

Too often we look upon daily life as routine, humdrum, uneventful, and we are ready to move on from a day's experiences, hoping that the future might hold something better. We may think that nothing extraordinary happened, so why look back?

We might be embarrassed by something foolish we did and just want to forget about it. That's where we can miss the opportunity to learn the lessons that that day is ready to teach us. While our missteps cannot be changed, going back over the day can provide the insight that will help us avoid the same mistakes in the future. Harmful habits are never broken by avoidance.

The technique for praying backward through the day is remarkably simple. To start, you might use these words from the Sacred Space website (www.sacredspace.ie):

> In God's loving presence I unwind the past day,
> starting from now and looking back, moment by moment.
> I gather in all the goodness and light, in gratitude.
> I attend to the shadows and what they say to me,
> seeking healing, courage, forgiveness.

Then work your way through the following prompts:

Beginning with the place you now are, the circumstances you find yourself in, let your mind rest for just a moment, realizing you are not alone.

Now let your mind slowly wander back through the day you have just lived. There is no hurry.

You may be surprised that you skip right over what seemed

to be the major events of the day and find yourself instead pondering the seemingly inconsequential.

Let your mind wander, let it take detours; that is exactly the purpose of this exercise.

If you find yourself making connections between something that happened today and something in the past, all the better. Most of us are creatures of habit. Our objective is to find those habits that enrich our well-being and those that are not in alignment with who we really are.

When you finally arrive at morning, rest again. Let the day's events speak to you.

Let those events of which you are proud confirm your desire to do them again or more often.

Consider those events that you know do not represent the best in you, and how you might better handle them in the future.

Here are three sample scenarios that illustrate praying backward through the day:

You are on a business trip and find yourself in a motel room. You think back to the clerk who checked you in and your attitude toward her. You think of the time you spent in a car or on a plane and what you did with that time. You might even reflect on some airport food you had and how you felt after eating. You think of the people you met, both those you knew and those you didn't. How did you conduct yourself? Did you feel whole or diminished by what you did and the people with whom you associated? Was there time to call a loved one? Is there a loved one? Did you take time to pray or meditate or simply sit still?

Praying backward through the day, like this entire book, is not an exercise in self-reproach or anxiety. Its purpose, rather, is to allow you to see yourself more clearly, to see where change is needed and where you are on track. Perhaps that fourth cup of coffee made you jittery and it is time to cut back. Perhaps you felt uneasy after a sales call, knowing that the person who made the presentation (you) is not the person you know yourself to be. Perhaps the happiness you felt in making the phone call to a loved one confirms the importance of that person in your life. Or perhaps the loneliness you felt forces you to admit that you are unsuccessfully using that person to fill a void.

It is finally time for bed and you are exhausted from the day, looking after a toddler and helping your grade-schooler with her homework. You were up early this morning, and it was a nonstop day, with little time to think about anything other than the meals, washing clothes, making sure you and your children were dressed and on time for school, playgroup, and activities. You made breakfast, lunch, supper. Well . . . that seems about it. Another routine day as a young parent?

Is each day just a blur of activity that feels stressful, or do you enjoy the nonstop quality of your life? Did you take time for yourself, or was that really necessary? How was your interaction with your children today: a case of "getting the job done" or enjoying some special moments? Was it overscheduled or just about the right balance between the planned and unplanned? What about your partner? What kind of interactions did you have with her or him?

You have looked forward to retirement, and here it is. It is one of the first days with no responsibilities, no decisions to make, nowhere you have to be at any special time.

Well, what kind of day was it, and what is going through your mind right now as you get ready for bed? Was the lack of responsibility satisfying or unsettling? Why do you think it was that way? What did you do this day, and how do you feel about how you used—or didn't use—your time? How does this day, only this day, fit into your idea of the kind of life you want to live, the kind of person you want to be?

4. LT3F or "Rummaging for God"

Almost twenty years ago, the Jesuit Dennis Hamm wrote about the LT3F approach—light, thanks, feelings, focus, future—which sounds quite contemporary but in fact represents the elements of the classic examen recommended by St. Ignatius. Father Hamm considers LT3F "rummaging for God" because it "suggests going through a drawer full of stuff, feeling around, looking for something that you are sure must be in there somewhere."

He notes that even before Christianity, the Pythagoreans and the Stoics promoted an examination of conscience to see how their daily behavior stacked up against the standards of their day. But he wants to expand that idea, moving from an examination of conscience—more or less what you did wrong—to a deeper sense of consciousness. In other words, he notes, "*consciousness* lets you cast your net much more broadly."

Here is a summary of Father Hamm's five-step approach:

Step 1. Pray for Light

We are not alone in this. God wants to help. We are not only trying to dredge up memories but what Father Hamm calls "graced understanding." You can pray in formal words or use those of Father Hamm: "Lord, help me understand this blooming, buzzing confusion."

Step 2. Review the Day in Thanksgiving

The idea is not to start immediately looking for your failures. What were the wonderful things that happened in the past twenty-four hours? Whom did you meet? What did you see that made you glad you were alive? For what gifts are you grateful?

Step 3. Reviewing the Day, What Feelings Are Evoked?

Don't try to put your feelings in a category; just let them surface, both positive and negative. Admit "the whole range: delight, boredom, fear, anticipation, resentment, anger, peace, contentment, impatience, desire, hope, regret, shame, uncertainty, compassion, disgust, gratitude, pride, rage, doubt, confidence, admiration, shyness—whatever was there," advises Father Hamm.

Step 4. Focus on a Feeling and Ponder It

> Again, don't try to be calculating by choosing something because it seems to be the "right" thing to think about. The strongest, most urgent feelings will point the way to where the "action" is in your life. Why did I feel this way? What happened before and after? What might it mean that I remember this feeling so vividly?

Step 5. Look Forward Toward the Future

> What does the next day bring—feelings of excitement or dread, confidence or questioning? Put yourself in God's presence and ask for whatever it is you need. You'll know what to request.

5. A Particular Examen

Perhaps there is one fault or habit that is especially plaguing you. A strong and effective spiritual practice called the particular examen could be very useful in both confronting whatever it is that weighs you down, and finding ways to release the burden.

What is my predominant fault?—temper, impatience, lust, greed, insensitivity, shallowness, arrogance . . . ? The list could

go on. You know the fault. Call it by name.

Think of the ways it negatively affects your life, your relationships, your physical and spiritual health, your job or vocation.

Decide that you want to change. You may do this in two ways:

First, practice the virtue that is the opposite of your fault. If it is your temper, practice patience. If it is arrogance, humility. Take small steps. For example, you are easily irritated—the morning commute, children thumping down the stairs, a coworker whose very voice has you boiling. Pause before honking, hollering, or heating up. Just take a deep breath. Allow your mind to move away to something positive—the flowers outside your car window, the love you have for your children, the efficient way your coworker does his or her job. By giving your best instincts a chance to work, you push your worst instincts to the background.

Second, do not give in to your fault, but, rather, practice your strongest virtue. You may be impatient, but you are a generous person. When ready to give in to your fault of, say, impatience, think of ways you have been generous. The Saturday meal you prepared at the homeless shelter, the check you wrote to help out an unemployed friend, the kind phone call you made to your mother. By reinforcing what you do well, you confirm your best instincts, and your faults no longer take center stage. In a sense, you forget to act upon them. You also run out of time to practice your faults if you're always practicing your virtues.

Certainly none of us changes with a single act. Our habits took a while to develop, and they will take time to be undeveloped. But the satisfaction that we sense in not responding to those bad instincts begins to have an impact. Quite simply, it feels better.

6. *Metta Bhavana:* **The Cultivation of Lovingkindness**

In our Western approach to examining our lives, we go at it directly: What am I doing wrong, what is bothering me, where am I failing, where, when and how am I acting contrary to the person I know myself to be?

The wisdom of the East looks at self-reflection and interior growth in a different and more oblique way and those who have found Buddhist meditation helpful might turn to the practice of *Metta Bhavana,* or the cultivation of lovingkindness, as their daily practice and way to embrace conscious living. These guided meditations concentrate not on faults or "sins," but turn the equation around, looking for the positive, the good, the potential, in ourselves and all beings. When a person understands and practices lovingkindness, the usual human tendencies that cripple us—selfishness, greed, impatience, lust—no longer have fertile ground within our minds to blossom into acts for which we will later be sorry.

Metta Bhavana is simple and can be practiced anytime, anywhere. Each step might take about five minutes, although there is no correct amount of time.

Step 1. Yourself

> Find a comfortable posture. It could be sitting or lying down. Take three very deep breaths, then return to breathing normally. Concentrate on each breath. Notice where you feel the breath most vividly—it could be the nostrils, the chest, or the abdomen. Rest your attention on this sensation. If your mind wanders off, gently bring it back to your breathing. Without judging or assessing, take note of your physical and mental state.

> Offer lovingkindness to yourself by saying silently, "May I be safe, may I be healthy, may I be happy, may I live with ease," or any wording that you feel more

comfortable with. Repeat the phrases inwardly, and try to gather your whole attention behind each phrase. The idea is to put your mind at rest.

Step 2. A benefactor or friend

Call up in your mind a person who has helped you or with whom you feel a deep kinship. Visualize this person and wish them well, send beams of light and good wishes into their lives and offer them the phrases of lovingkindness: "May you be safe, may you be healthy, may you be happy, may you live with ease." You may find that negative feelings mix in with the good thoughts you have about that person. Accept them and allow them to pass away as your attention focuses on the repetition of the phrases. Continue imagining good things for your benefactor.

Step 3. A "neutral" person

Now bring to mind someone you see often but never think about, like a clerk in a store. Extend those same positive thoughts and good wishes to this person: "May you be safe, be healthy, be happy, live with ease." Figuratively stand beside them. Reach out, take their hand.

In this step, you have moved beyond your self-interest, outside your circle of friends and family. You begin to realize that everyone in the human family seeks happiness and kindness, no one in the human family wants to suffer, or to feel alone, unwanted.

Step 4. Someone you dislike

Now, go further. Imagine someone with whom you are having a problem. Someone who may not have your best interest at heart; someone who may have hurt you, or continues to hurt you. This will probably be more difficult, as it may call up negative feelings. This is not an exercise in forgiving others, or in condoning their bad behavior. It is simply to enter their lives for a few moments and stand with them in solidarity, two frail human beings, each so different, yet, like all beings, each wanting to be happy. It is here that we try to see that person's point of view, to understand that their actions may come from deep-seated pain. We send them our wishes for their peace of mind. "May you be peaceful, may you be free of suffering and the causes of suffering, may you be happy."

Step 5. The entire universe

Now, expand your awareness to all living beings. Let your mind sweep across oceans, skim over mountain ranges, into the lives of all those who inhabit the earth, the animals, the fish, the birds, microorganisms. Imagine yourself as the sun, radiating out from where you sit, warming each person, animal, and place. Send your good wishes, your consolation, your fervent wish that all would be well, everywhere: "May all beings be safe, may all beings be happy, may all beings be healthy, may all beings live with ease." At this very moment, there are no boundaries, no limitations.

Sit, rest, and allow your mind to be at peace. Breathe deeply in . . . and out. When you are ready, rise up and go about your life. Now, as best you can, bring lovingkindness with you into your day.

7. An Adult Examination of Conscience

Those of us who come from religious traditions that asked us to periodically measure our behavior against a set of rules or mandates (like the Ten Commandments) can well remember the "laundry list" school of confession. Did I disobey my parents? How many times? Did I steal? How much?

This exacting approach may or may not have helped shape our moral character. I believe that, didactic as it was, it did us more good than harm. Probably we were better children because we knew which lines we could not cross.

We are now adults. We have lived enough of our lives to keep small infractions in perspective, knowing that to keep meticulous account of every little lie or selfishness is not really living consciously, but rather, neurotically. What we seek to know are the habits, tendencies, actions, reactions, and inactions that make our lives and our relationships whole or hollow, life-giving or moribund.

The idea is not to go through the following list in its entirety at any one time. Rather, start anywhere and ponder the question as long as it is beneficial in examining yourself, your motives, and the results.

1. Daily Life

Have I

Given my best effort to the opportunities offered me?
Been awake to the many blessings I have received?
Known when anger was justified and when it was not?
Spoken up when I should have; listened when needed?
Looked upon others as objects to exploit?
Stood with people who needed my support?

Acted arrogantly?

Lost my temper unnecessarily?

2. Work

Have I

Used my talents to their highest calling?

Seen the possibilities and integrity in even the
simplest tasks?

Been a good team player?

Sought not just my own good, but when possible,
the larger good?

Aspired to do my best?

Settled for mediocrity?

Betrayed myself to get ahead?

Put work ahead of family and friends?

3. Desires

Have I

Looked beyond immediate goals or accomplishments
to what is truly important in life?

Been able to see the value in my failures?

Sought good not only for myself, but for others?

Acted on physical desire, the pleasure of the moment,
regardless of consequences?

Needed to be acclaimed for everything I do?

Envied the success of others?

Allowed ambition to rule my life?

4. Inner Life

Have I

Taken time to reflect on my life?

Listened to those voices in my life that I know to be
trustworthy?

Been able to assess which influences are good for me?

Been honest with myself when faced with
tough decisions?

5. Physical Well-Being

Have I

Eaten healthy food?

Exercised?

Been reasonable about my intake of alcohol?

Stopped those habits I know are harmful to my body?

Treated my body like the holy temple that it is?

Made my body an obsession?

Dressed in a way that honored my body?

Treated my sexuality with respect?

Treated others as sexual objects?

6. Loving

Have I

Given myself freely to those dear to me?

Used my love as a bargaining chip, to get my way?

Tried to love the unlovable people in my life?

Loved only because I wanted to be loved in return?

Mistaken my selfish jealousy for honest love?

7. Personal Integrity

Have I

Betrayed trusts or those who have trusted in me?

Tried to rationalize my way out of difficult decisions
I had to make?

Overlooked minor but consistent breaches of honesty?

Cheated or lied when I knew I could get away with it?

Made excuses for my poor behavior instead of trying to
change it?

8. Relationships

Have I

Been a good friend?

Reached out to friends when they needed me?

Worked to deepen healthy relationships?

Worked to end relationships I know are unhealthy for me?

Made it difficult for others to love me?

Looked down on or ignored people different from me?

Made commitments casually, knowing I would
   break them?

Honored my commitment as wife, husband, partner?

Been able to put myself in another's situation, to better
   understand that person?

9. Spiritual Life

Have I

Prayed or meditated recently and regularly?

Taken time alone?

Examined my life, my motives?

Kept myself so busy there is no time to reflect?

Trusted that God loves and cares for me?

10. Nature

Have I

Been a good steward of the earth's resources?

Used only those resources I needed?

Reused older items that were perfectly good rather than
   buying new ones?

Spent time in nature?

Looked about me in wonder at the beauty of creation?

11. Money/Possessions

Do I

Sacrifice core principles to make more money?

Know the difference between want and need?

Use money well, being neither a spendthrift nor a miser?

Make more, or less, than I need for a healthy, balanced life?

Own my possessions, or do they own me?

Spend money on things I don't need?

Spend money to fill a void rather than confronting the void?

You will find yourself comforted by those questions whose answers come quickly—these are not issues in your life. And then there will be a question that will give you pause. So pause. Reflect. Then think about how you might act differently.

Remember: The exercises offered in this chapter are not meant to be a ledger sheet to catalog your good and bad deeds, hoping to come out with a plus, not minus, balance. They are simply tools to help you see yourself honestly and thereby to practice living honestly every day.

It sounds so simple, but we all know the difficulty we have in being honest about ourselves. It's hard to form good, useful habits, and begin to change and make those midlife corrections.

confessing

How, What, to Whom, Where (and When Not To)

WHAT DO WE do with what we have discovered about ourselves? The little murders we have committed, trusts betrayed, destructive habits continued, intimacies cheapened? Shall we make amends to the people we have hurt? To the God we have offended? To our best selves we've betrayed?

In short, how do we know when it is time to confess?

The answer might seem simple: anytime we have consciously wronged ourselves or another person, place, or thing. But life brings us complicated situations and decisions and it's not always apparent what to do about them.

Whatever form our confessions take, they ought not to be the product of dogged, unreflective rule-following; nor, on the other hand, should we recuse ourselves with elegant bouts of rationalizing: "The devil made me do it." "Everybody does it, so why should I be different?" "How can you hold me responsible for my actions when . . ." If we filter our actions through a litany of excuses, nothing remains to confess.

CONFESSION'S THREE Rs: RISK, RELIEF, RENEWAL

"Like the pilgrim, the patient, in confessing, comes gradually to rediscover the essence of the true self. Yet, this discovery rarely, if ever, involves a one-trial learning experience," writes Sharon Hymer in *Confessions in Psychotherapy.* "The patient who takes the first step—risk—immediately makes a major advance in peeling away the layers of the false self." And indeed, confession is often spoken of as comprising three Rs—risk, relief, and renewal.

We seek—who would not?—the last two Rs of this trilogy, relief and renewal. The problem is the first. How wonderful it would be if one led seamlessly to the next; in other words, if freshness and clarity would be ours once we have taken the risk of unburdening ourselves of something that has haunted us.

The risk can be great, which is why confession tends not to be a spontaneous act, but something we mull over and over, assessing the consequences: What will people think of me? Will I be able to face them in the future? What will the fallout be? Often it is only when need outbalances fear that we are ready to risk confessing.

Virtually every confession we make will touch these three points, but rarely is it a straight path.

RISK

We tend to "stick to prior decisions and attempt to justify them rather than having to admit mistakes and incur losses. The more one follows this course," write Wilkie and Noreen Au, "the more one invests in the original decision and feels entrapped by it." Behavioral economists have studied the phenomenon from a business perspective, finding that the more money a company has sunk into a failing product, the more funds it is likely to continue to shovel over the problem rather than admit defeat. The only way to stop the cycle is to go back to the source of the original misjudgment.

Usually, the greater the violation, the greater the risk involved. The deeper the intimacy, the greater the potential fallout in presenting our flawed selves to a loved one. It is the leap of faith into unknown consequences that most often keeps people from owning up to their actions. We might be abandoned. We might lose the trust of someone we love. Friendship may go. We may look like a fool. Our sense of self-worth might be diminished. As long as we keep the offending act or secret to ourselves we can at least pretend it either doesn't exist or is inconsequential. Once we confess it, the mask is off and there we are.

The risk of confession is why so many bartenders and cab drivers hear the most intimate secrets. They are low-risk outlets, usually strangers with no link to the confessant's life. At times, they hear "practice confessions," a testing of the waters: If this stranger isn't shocked, maybe we can confess to the person actually involved.

It would be foolish to set up Rules of Risk, of what a person should confess and to whom, as if this were some business school exercise in perceived profit and potential loss. Life is too fluid, circumstances and reactions too unpredictable for that. We all carry varying layers of self-defense; some of us have more self-cohesion and will be better able to weather the fallout of a momentous confession. Some of us have had horrible experiences with being honest in the past and have vowed never to expose ourselves again.

All we can do is return to the need/fear equation. When need becomes overwhelming, when what we are holding back is negatively affecting the lives of others or damaging our own, crippling us emotionally as we keep up pretenses, it is time to risk disclosure.

Another way of looking at the element of risk is to substitute another R word: responsibility. Confession is the unique human act in which a person, on his or her own initiative, evaluates actions and, finding some of them not up to personal standards, religious codes, or the public order, makes the choice to reveal that failure.

Risk is responsibility. Responsibility is bravery.

RELIEF

The problem we have been hiding is exposed and can haunt us no more.

Here is where the art of living honestly pays its quiet but considerable benefit. Certainly our problem cannot grow. It must leave center stage, even be sent out the door, where we can view it from a distance with a mixture of pain, relief, and perhaps even amusement. The foundation upon which we may have built a fragile network of elaborate lies crumbles from disuse. Guilt's obsessive, repetitive inward focus may fade away.

The relief resulting from our confession allows us to at once own our actions and distance ourselves from them.

Rather than give in to the fault, claiming it is a force outside us we can't control, we acknowledge it and integrate it into our full being. Do we then walk the face of the earth as totally good human beings, this evil exterminated once and for all? Of course not; we know what we have done. We may do it again.

Renewal

Is renewal guaranteed once we take the risk of honesty? I wish it were.

While confession usually brings an initial sense of relief, our revelation may in fact have some negative consequences, usually by bringing to the surface a situation that was quietly lying dormant beneath our blanket of deceit. Living out the reality of a "firm purpose of amendment" means just that. I have to change my behavior and that change can be painfully difficult. Our life situation might get worse before it gets better, but the hope (and usually the end result) is that even though we may suffer through embarrassment, personal agony, and loss of love or friendship, we will be able to move through to wholeness once more. The loss we sustain, and it may be great, will eventually be outweighed by equilibrium's return.

One of the true gifts of risking confession is that we can often go deeper and work through an underlying problem. Take the example of a man who was sexually unresponsive to his wife. Over the years he blamed her: She was not interested in sex, she had gained weight, she always complained of being tired . . . the classic scenarios. But finally, he told her that as a teenager, his father had found him fondling another boy and beat him severely. It was only the innocent act of two pubescent boys, probing and testing their sexuality, but he'd felt dirty about sex ever since. Moreover, he confessed, he'd projected his feelings onto his wife, in reality a compassionate, sensual woman.

He felt initial relief at his confession but was then overwhelmed with embarrassment. For a while, intimacy seemed even more tentative, but as he and his wife talked through their various early sexual experiences, good and bad, they were able to come to a new and better understanding of each other. His wife made it clear that she forgave him and that there was nothing he needed to be embarrassed about. Their love for each other began to deepen and blossom, and their physical attraction for each other took on new and richer dimensions.

WHEN TO CONFESS

Though there is no rule for determining whether a confession is necessary, here's one way to think about it: If we have deeply offended someone or violated a trust or have, in the myriad ways we all sin, either taken what wasn't ours or selfishly held back what we should have given, we may want to communicate that.

To help you decide, try asking yourself the following questions:

Did I do, and am I still doing, something wrong? What do I need to do to make it right?

Did I intend—consciously or unconsciously—to commit this action? If I did, I must take responsibility for it and confess, make restitution, or transform a habit. If I did not intend the action, was it the result of negligence, a lack of attention? If so, perhaps that is what I need to address, whether I make a firm purpose of amendment within myself or choose to articulate it to someone else.

Looking beyond the surface of my actions, what was I really thinking, feeling, hoping would occur because of what I did? What am I really thinking, feeling, hoping will occur as a result of my confession?

Face-to-face, by phone, letter, or e-mail—there are many ways to communicate one's wrong to another. Some of us can better explain ourselves when we put pen to paper or digits to keyboard. Sometimes nothing short of sitting down with a person will do. You know the wrong; you will sense the best way to confess and to make amends.

There are other times—far, far more numerous—when what we have done needs to be acknowledged within us but nowhere else. This may sound like a cop-out, but in fact, for many, the internal confession is the hardest and the most meaningful one of all. And it would be foolish to constantly attempt to narrate the little faults we all commit. Perhaps you have a least favorite, long-winded brother-in-law, and at the last family reunion, you hardly disguised your dislike. Your sister was crushed; he is her husband, after all, and she dreads the next time the three of you will be in the same room. Instead of an apology, just appearing at the next family reunion, listening to one of his meandering monologues and smiling before going back for another hamburger might be the perfect solution. Dishonest? I don't think so. Just practical. Your actions do speak louder than the words you might have offered.

I thought about this the other morning as I was getting some shaving gel out of the aerosol can. I pressed the cap too hard and wound up with far more than I could use. I stood there dumbly. How could I rectify my error of judgment? Of course, I couldn't squeeze it back into the aerosol can. All I

From Dr. Thomas Mathew

LISTENING TO A CONFESSION

In psychotherapy we can treat outward symptoms—depression, anxiety, ennui—with medication, which sometimes is very effective in itself. Sometimes medication can grease the skids so that a person can feel better enough to go deeper, to the causes. In fact, many people come to us not looking for confession but for Prozac. Don't get me wrong, modern antidepressants are a miracle. But they also can be the bandage over a gaping wound that you might cover for the moment; true healing will never occur until the infection is found and cleansed.

From a therapeutic point of view, to really come to an understanding of these deeper wounds, we need something quite simple: time. Time builds trust; time allows a person to go deeper. Just as a therapist should never condemn or offer quick, succinct solutions, neither should a friend or acquaintance when listening to someone being honest about his problems, for this just ends the dialogue and leaves the person alone with his or her misery. Do not judge; that always shuts down a confession. And don't jump in with a solution.

Just listen.

could do was wash it down the drain and resolve to be more alert the next time.

A very ordinary example, for certain. But sometimes there is no "getting the toothpaste back into the tube." We simply need to see what we've done and resolve to do better. Life will present enough times for true confession; we don't have to look for opportunities when the offense is minuscule.

To Whom Should I Confess?

Often we have known too long and too well *what* we have done, or we have finally discovered it through thoughtful and honest introspection. Now where do we go with this burden or revelation? It is important to see as clearly as we can to whom we should be confessing.

Our decision becomes easier (though not necessarily easy) and clearer (though not necessarily clear) if we look within and, as best we can, decide:

Is this a moral issue—sin in the classic religious sense?

Is this an offense against the common good, a higher power, God?

Is this a psychological issue—continuing, self-inflicted, and harmful behavior?

Is this a social, interpersonal issue, an offense against another person?

Of course, our actions or habits can incorporate elements from each of these realms. A predatory and deceitful sexual life is a perfect example; compulsive lying, another. Where to go to confess will vary from person to person, but if we can see who it is we have offended or wronged, then we know where to go for reconciliation.

Let us consider an example.

You and your friend went to the same college, have known each other for years, and have become close friends. You now work for the same IT company as managers.

Throughout your life, although you have tried to stop a habit of jealousy over the accomplishments of others, you have not fared so well. You talk disparagingly of those who are successful or acclaimed; the newspaper provides a perfect daily outlet for you to criticize public officials, media and entertainment celebrities, even "do-gooders" in your own city. So when your friend becomes one of the finalists for the elite, new-initiatives research group at work but you do not, your jealousy knows no bounds.

You dredge up all the negative stories about your friend that you can remember, and even enhance them. You casually drop the stories into conversations with coworkers. You tell of college drinking and drugs. You tell about skirting the edges of honesty with some assignments. Your friend has just confided in you that there is trouble at home; you make sure your supervisor knows about those difficulties. The office knows your friend as a top-notch employee, competent and cooperative. The picture you paint is of an unstable, unreliable, less than honest person.

The final selection is made. Your friend is not chosen.

Now you feel horribly guilty. What to do? There are generally three types of confessions available to you.

Religious Confession

In all major religious traditions, to slander another person, to denigrate someone unfairly, to be jealous, or to covet is considered an offense, a sin.

Is this a time to see a rabbi, priest, or minister or to acknowledge this fault in a religious service or ritual? It might be. You have not only affected your friend's future, you have belittled yourself and the generosity of God, who looks upon all creatures with compassion and love, and shares in their triumphs.

Psychological Confession

This kind of jealousy is not a passing blip on the screen of your life. Looking at it honestly, you can see that it is deep-seated and ultimately unproductive. It poisons your outlook.

It will not help you become a more successful person. Nor will it help you become a contented person who sees in life enough opportunity to go around, rather than a miser so absorbed in counting the slices in the pie that he cannot enjoy the pie at all. There will always be someone of whom you can be envious. And jealousy is not a pleasant state of mind.

You will have to decide if you want to continue to live this way or if you want to seek professional, therapeutic help in changing your outlook.

Personal Confession

Should you go to your friend and confess or go on as if you had no part in the outcome? Your random and unkind comments may have had little or no bearing on the choice. But in your heart, you know—and will always know—that your jealousy rose up, roaring out of the depths of your being and devouring anything in its path.

In this hypothetical case, one or all of these avenues to "righting" oneself may be needed. You may need to tell God you have sinned, the therapist that you have this self-destructive habit, your friend that you betrayed the friendship.

Or perhaps there is someone else to whom you can go and confide. Perhaps that is exactly what you will do, and perhaps it will be enough.

You will not find the right answer here. You will find it in your heart.

From Dr. Thomas Mathew

A RELEASE FOR WRONGFUL GUILT

When people begin treatment in a therapist's office, they surely have made a significant first step in facing and hopefully solving the issues that are making them unhappy. But they still want to be seen in the best possible light. And they do not yet know if they can really trust you. So you will receive a muted version, veiled confession. An example I remember well from my time as a medical resident was the story a young female EMT shared on admission to the psychiatric unit where I was working. She had been admitted for feeling depressed and suicidal.

We could call those symptoms a "confession in themselves," and it is not hard to see that these are but surface effects of a deep inner conflict. After a short time, the EMT revealed to me that when she was young, she had been sexually abused by her father. She had never confronted him about this. As an adult health care professional, she found herself in the extraordinarily difficult position of being in his house when he suffered a massive heart attack. She had to give him CPR and call 911. He died.

She had not told anyone about this but felt guilty for years because she wasn't sure she had given her best effort to save his life. Because of this guilt she carried around—the guilt that she may have allowed her father to die—she made a suicide attempt.

I'm still not sure why she picked me to confess to, except that I shared with her that I was a spiritual seeker like herself. This, in some way, freed her to trust me with her confession.

The confession seemed to be quite cathartic for her. Her suicidal depression resolved without medication, and she was eager to move forward spiritually, connecting and becoming involved with a faith community I told her about.

Twenty years later, she found me on the Internet and sent me a very nice letter, thanking me for hearing her "confession" and going on to tell me about her spiritual and psychological growth since. This simple and yet profound act began a wonderful downstream cascade of psychological benefits.

Do Secret Confessions Work?

Anyone who has sat in a therapist's office or in a confessional booth—or today, confessed online—knows that a private, perhaps anonymous revelation of our failings can still be a wrenching experience.

Some would argue that these are not true confessions, that they may be helpful in the short term but they do not get at the root of the problem and will not help you change self-destructive habits and actions.

It's easy to laugh and thumb our noses at the confessional iPhone app—so far removed from the realms of human connection in which our moral and emotional contracts are forged—but there is an argument to be made for the safety afforded by privacy. Catholic Confession, after all, occurs in a darkened booth for a reason. And how many stories I have heard of the person who walks in off the street, confesses to a priest, and has a life-changing encounter. "Several months ago, I found myself in your confessional after 40 years of living a sinful life. The mercy and forgiveness . . . completely changed the direction of my life," a man wrote to Father Fergus Healey, after he'd stepped off busy Arch Street in Boston and into St. Anthony Shrine.

Sometimes, minimizing the risk attached to our confessions is the way forward. The teenager who confesses to a stranger that she or he is an alcoholic takes little risk, but confessing this to a teetotaling parent is an enormous risk. That stranger may provide the first step in recovering that teenager's life. Likewise, though they took place within the security of confidentiality, I would never say that my confessions during four years of Jungian analysis were not beneficial; in fact, they were critical in my being able to see myself clearly, stop destructive behavior, and set out on a better path in life.

Secret confessions may be exactly what is needed. Each individual will have to judge for herself or himself, but I offer a few simple guidelines for other types of confessions.

If what you have done can be told—confessed—to a trusted friend, a clergyperson, or a therapist, or even perhaps simply acknowledged by you, then you need do no more; that is enough.

If you have hurt or offended someone and if it will be resolved only by telling that person directly what you have done and of your sorrow, then tell them. The person may already know what you did, but saying it directly leaves no unfinished issues, freeing both of you to acknowledge it and move on.

Confess selectively. Confess only to those people whose opinion matters to you or who were directly affected by your actions. Remember: Sharing promiscuously dilutes feeling, and even a truly felt sentiment too often repeated becomes rote. Maintain the meaning in your words. Drunkenly informing a group of strangers that you've cheated on your husband is no sign of a fresh start.

Let your confession be neither an attempt at assuaging your guilt by seeking corroboration for your actions ("I did it, but so do you, don't you?") nor a further act of aggression, inflicting unnecessary hurt.

WHEN *NOT* TO CONFESS

Should we confess directly to those we have hurt? A telling and unexpected answer came from a priest I know. One of his parishioners asked for an appointment. After the office door was closed, the man revealed that he had had an extended affair. It was over, had been over for a while, but the guilt haunted him. He loved his wife, loved his children. He wanted to stay married, but he just couldn't go on bearing this terrible secret. He had to tell his wife, so that he could put it behind him.

I was surprised at the priest's response. "Don't tell her," the priest told the man bluntly. "What would that prove or do, except devastate her? Keep this as your own secret; live with it. It will be a stone in your shoe, a constant reminder of what you did. So you will never be tempted to do it again."

Confessing to the afflicted party can actually be an act of cruelty. Your weight of guilt may be lifted. You'll feel relieved. But who suffers now? As my priest friend clarified later, "If this was a moral lapse, and not a habit, I think keeping it to himself is the right remedy. If this is just one in a string of infidelities or something the person knows will happen again, then to be honest with himself and his spouse, it has to be revealed."

Whatever our choice, few of us will ever have to face television cameras or huge crowds as we confess that we have violated a trust, hurt someone, or broken a law. But the principles separating apology from confession, rationalization from honesty, and blaming from taking responsibility do not change because of who we are. In our lives, on our own stages, we will have many opportunities to put on a show rather than come clean.

As there is a big difference between the letter of the law and the spirit of the law, there can be an equally wide chasm between our confessing a mistake and actually being fully honest about it—both to a possible offended party and, even more important, to ourselves. We might apologize to a fellow employee—"Oh, sorry I spoke out of turn at the meeting. I should keep my big mouth shut"—meanwhile concealing that the reason we did it was to cut the person off and impress the boss.

It is so much better to say: "I'm sorry I interrupted you—it was selfish of me and disrespectful toward you. It won't happen again." Simple. Painful. And exactly what we need to do.

From Sister Karen Kirby

LOOKING FOR SOLACE

It's a little hard for people to blurt out in a supermarket, "My life is going to hell and I don't know what to do about it"—even in some church offices, so I've been told. But standing in front of the Health and Wellness section of the bookstore, it happens all the time. I usually know when they walk in. No eye contact. They are not quite there. I let them be by themselves for a while; then I go over and ask, "Is there anything special you're looking for?"

Of course, they are looking for someone to talk to, someone to whom they can unburden themselves. I feel so lucky to work where I do. The bookstore offers a safe, unthreatening place. You don't have to say up front "I am in trouble and I need help." You can just kind of slide into it.

There was a woman—later on I would find out that her husband was beating her, but even without marks you could see she was wounded. It was her fault, she confessed to me. She wasn't a good enough mother or wife. She had gone to her parish priest, and he told her that her duty was to her husband, regardless. She just had to try harder.

Probably in desperation she ended up in the bookstore, and yes, I can suggest some self-help book, but it's more than that. I think I can apply the balm of understanding to her wounds.

do the next right thing

Shaping a New Way of Living

WHETHER WE WHISPER our disclosures to our inner accountant or announce them in a more formal admission of wrongdoing, what happens after our confessions is the most important part. Even with the best of intentions to change our patterns of behavior, of acting or reacting without thought or concern, we may, and very likely will, fall and fail again, giving in to our worst instincts, making the same mistakes, inflicting the same hurts. To say that we will *never* repeat our mistakes is to feel good for an instant but to condemn ourselves to a legacy of lying. We will grind those well-meaning intentions of the moment into dust.

Here's a more realistic and optimistic scenario:
Our failings, even our most horrible failings, if properly
acknowledged and understood, can serve as sea buoys we
put in place after running aground too many times on the
shoals of misguided actions. These buoys will, in the future,
mark the safe channel of our activities. When we go outside
the buoys, and we can at any time, we will know we are
headed for trouble.

On a daily basis, you, a fluid, changing, conflicted
individual, hear the beckoning call of your particular angels
and demons. Your response depends on where you are in
life, sometimes even on the time of day. But the principles
that make up your moral realm remain. The sea buoys of
your experiences will guide you. Do not look too far down
the channel. Just stay between the buoys of this day, this
experience, and you will be on a safe course.

A FIRM PURPOSE OF AMENDMENT

The phrase "a firm purpose of amendment" comes from the
bedrock of my religious tradition, but it took me decades to
understand—and years more to employ. As a young person,
it hovered over my head and my actions like a guillotine
set to drop at the slightest moral relapse. Just typing the
characters still brings a twinge of guilt.

That amendment part was the hitch in our weekly confessional sacrament. We were taught to prepare for Confession by carefully going down the list of possible offenses against God, but we were admonished *not* to confess a sin unless we were willing to make a firm purpose to mend our ways and not commit that sin again. If we were not ready to change, there was little use in admitting what we had done.

Logically running this out, by the time children reached puberty, they had gone out of their minds with guilt, were ready to be canonized as saints, or had simply given up the whole business of morality as utterly impossible.

I was a normal teenager, with normal teenage impulses. To promise (and I guess I did) that I would never participate in some hot necking, as we used to call it, in the backseat of my brother's Ford at that dark parking spot on the shore at Cleveland's Shaker Lake, was to lie, week after week. It is, after all, sins of the flesh that occupy many of our wishes and much of the incumbent guilt during our teenage years. Thankfully, our repertoire expands as we grow older.

As teenagers, we had to use some sort of subterfuge to get through, and we did. We convinced ourselves that by sheer will and self-control we could suppress testosterone and the other hormones, be mystically transformed into

From Father Steven LaBaire

LISTENING TO YOUR LIFE

Some Catholics bemoan the fact that Confession went out of popularity. The reason the bottom fell out, almost overnight, is that it didn't add up. It didn't make sense. You miss Mass once and you go to hell?

Here was the exchange: The penitent gives me the list. I give the penitent prayers to say and pronounce my magical incantation over her, and she goes back into the world. Does that person understand any better why she did what she did? The emphasis was in all the wrong places. In our Catholic education, especially before Vatican II, we were told we were sinful. In Confession we were made to say we would never do any bad things again.

Most of us are not that strong. We will sin again. But incrementally, we can do better. That is what I encourage people to do: just a firm resolve to do their best. Not to be perfect. Do their best.

Now, a person can come to the Sacrament of Reconciliation (the new incarnation of Confession) or he can just tell me what is troubling him. I offer support and perhaps a pathway out of behavior that is harming him or his loved ones. I can give advice. But more often I help people call on their own resources. They know what is right and good. To find that, we need to pray. Prayer is listening to your life. And when you listen to your life, you know what to do.

angels, and never again have such physical desires. Of course, we were fooling ourselves.

As I grew older and saw my own patterns of weakness, I began to realize that no one benefited from my wallowing in my wrongdoings. If my "firm purpose of amendment" might help to shape my future life, it had to keep one foot firmly in reality, even as the other reached for higher ground.

ARTICULATING THE CHANGE WE SEEK

In bridging the gap between that elusive high ground and our sometimes muddy daily dwelling place, here are some considerations I've found it useful to ponder:

How might my "firm purpose of amendment" be reasonably stated? What is a step toward a more honest way of life and away from the kind of behavior that I want to change?

How firm is my purpose of amendment? Am I facing myself and my actions honestly or am I fooling myself and making excuses?

Let's take an example. I am overweight. I travel frequently and can't control my eating. I am a binge eater. Alone in a hotel room, I gorge, convincing myself that I deserve some pleasure after a tough day. But even on easy days, I do the same. My physician has told me that if I do not lose weight, I am a candidate for a heart attack. I look at myself in the mirror and I am appalled. I used to have a reasonably healthy body—never that athletic or that thin, but nothing like this. I have abused my body; I have sinned against myself. By shortening my life span, I'm not acting responsibly toward my spouse or my children. I have to rest walking up stairs. I can't play with my children without gasping or even go out with friends on those walks I used to love. This must stop. My firm purpose of amendment is to lose weight by joining Overeaters Anonymous.

What is a reasonable step toward a more honest way of life and away from this kind of behavior? What is my individual firm purpose of amendment? Am I making excuses, or am I facing myself and my actions honestly?

I'm fooling myself if:

I convince myself that this was really a tough day and I deserve any pleasure at hand.

I tell myself I'm not that overweight. Look, with this suit on, you can barely tell I've gained thirty pounds.

I argue that I'm a normal weight because the Time *magazine article I just read said that the average American is seventeen pounds overweight.*

I'm facing myself if I realize that:

Yes, it was a tough day, but this pleasure is going to be short-lived and ultimately not healthy for me.

Yes, I am overweight, and it shows.

The actions of the "average American" are not an appropriate barometer for what is right for me. I am overweight. I don't want to be.

Instead of an Internet search for a pizza parlor that will deliver to the hotel, I look up the local OA chapter. I try to make a meeting. If I can't, I put in a call to my OA sponsor. Instead of getting a half gallon of ice cream from the deli next door to the hotel, I get a Popsicle and order a good movie. I make sure I'll be at the next OA meeting when I get home.

Do the Next Right Thing

Although I write about the spiritual life, I tried very hard not to preach to my sons as they were growing up. I was never very good at changing my life patterns when admonished by adults, and I didn't want to inflict fruitless chastisement or unhelpful truisms on my children. Instead, I told them what I told anyone who was guilt-ridden and asked me for guidance: "Do the next right thing."

It's easy to see from the Overeaters Anonymous example what might be involved in an attempt to do the next right thing. Dramatic? Not always. And yet . . . possible. One step in the right direction.

We could all fill in examples from our own lives—habits we want to change, past offenses we want to right. We might fall back into a habit of drinking too much, snapping into a rage for little reason, sharing juicy bits of gossip we know to be but half-truths. We could say we drank because we were happy, sad, triumphant, defeated—all of us drinkers have a ready arsenal of excuses; that we grew angry because of someone else's stupid or insensitive actions; or that we gossiped because, well, she or he deserved it and this half-truth was probably pretty close to the whole truth anyhow.

There is no automatic Off switch to eradicate the habits of a defensive mind accustomed to subterfuge, nor is there an automatic switch for virtue. Any change is accomplished in increments and with practice. As we hone our ability to look squarely at our actions and own up to what we have done and not done, we move forward, albeit sometimes slowly. And each day brings the potential for living more in keeping with our professed values.

As an example of how events work upon those of us who are yet to mature spiritually, let me tell you about a recent, rainy morning when I was going into my local YMCA for my daily swim.

There she stood, near the entrance, bedraggled, soaking, shivering. A prostitute? Drug addict? Whatever the case, it was obvious to see that hers had been a hard life. She asked for a ride.

And what did I do?—Paul Wilkes, who started a storefront in Brooklyn to care for the street people, who started a foundation to rescue and educate slum girls in India? Umbrella in hand, carefully protected from rain, I nodded and walked right past her.

On lap six that morning, the parable of the Good Samaritan flashed into my mind. Same situation, two thousand years earlier. Just like those folks, I passed by. I felt horrible as I thought about what I had done, or rather, not done. I mentioned it to a friend who said (kindly—he knew how guilty I felt), "Things like that happen for a purpose."

If I was worried about my own safety—which I was—I could have offered her a few dollars for a cab ride. I could have given her my umbrella. I had three more at home. I failed her and I failed myself. I did not act in accordance with what was best in me. I was guilty, but I was not condemned. Maybe it did happen for a purpose. The next time will be different.

Virtue for the Unvirtuous

In talking with clergy and therapists about the people who come to them and confess, I heard the same sentiments over and over again: People are tougher on themselves than anyone else would be; and beneath their flaws or their flawed actions, they have very good instincts. As one parish priest said:

"People who come to me want to know they are not as evil as some people might think they are—not as evil as they might even judge themselves. They are not asking me to condone what they have done. They want to come clean, to let someone know. They need to say it out loud. They have done something bad; they want to know they are not bad people. In fact, they are not bad people. They are far better people than they give themselves credit for."

Connecting with those instincts is our task. Sister Helen Prejean, renowned for her work with death row prisoners (and her bestselling book, *Dead Man Walking,* which was made into a movie), admits she had no idea what she was undertaking when she responded to a handwritten, grammatically errant letter from death row prisoner Matthew Poncelet. She would go on to accompany him to execution, as she would for many others after, and become a powerful advocate for the abolition of the death penalty. Sister Prejean had no grand plan; she only had, as she often recalls in her speeches, a "little flashlight" that helped her to see what the next step should be.

So it is in our lives. We are not given powerful searchlights to peer far into the future, so that we see exactly where we are going and what we need to do to get there, never straying from the path. Within each of us is that little flashlight, divinely implanted, that allows us to see our present moment. And within us is that magnificent moral compass, our conscience, the very seat of our soul, the point at which the divine touches the human, providing the guidance for that next step. Our conscience "sees." Our conscience weighs. Our conscience bids us to act in this way and not that.

Certainly many of life's situations are confusing, offering a dizzying array of options. We change, situations change, our culture shifts. What once might have been considered horrible becomes repugnant. Repugnant becomes reasonably acceptable. Reasonably acceptable becomes absolutely permissible. But amid all this fluidity, our responses can be guided by something beyond our reason or society's mores, a divine wellspring of insight and good judgment.

Virtue is not an end product, a result, a final reckoning. It is a daily effort to see more clearly, act more justly. And what a gift it is to see it this way.

afterword

"A MOMENT COMES, WHICH comes but rarely . . . , when we step out from the old and into the new." Jawaharlal Nehru's words, as India threw off its colonial past and became an independent nation in 1947, had to do with change on the grandest of scales. But in them we can recognize the image of a human being stepping out of an old suit of clothes and into a wholly new possibility. And so it is with confession. Changing our thinking, our behavior, developing confessional awareness may be gradual, but confession can allow for powerful moments of transformation.

One who has unburdened herself or himself of a deception or betrayal or come clean about a complicity may have known such a moment. The first step taken in a new direction can mark a turning point in one's life, with a distinct before and after. These are moments that transform our thinking, attitude, hopes—sometimes even our posture—as if a great weight has been lifted.

Insight Is What We Seek

Søren Kierkegaard, the existentialist often remembered for his dark forays into angst and depression, would seem an unlikely cheerleader for a practice of introspection laced with optimism. But the philosopher, theologian, and fledgling psychologist was a proponent of "purity of heart," a state he set in contrast with empty rituals, proper prayers uttered without thought. It was not enough to tend to the surface traits, habits, and practices of one's life. The truly "existing" person should be willing to plunge deeper, to find and to live a life's purpose. Dormant possibilities could never be realized without the ability to look inward. It's interesting that to strip away pretense, Kierkegaard saw the need to block out the world's judgment-clouding "noise," busyness, and "double-mindedness."

The point is that the sense of well-being that confession imparts is only a beginning. Emotional release is but a first—and sometimes fleeting—reward. On the deeper plane, insight and wisdom are what we seek.

There is no confessional time-release pill that will miraculously portion out its healing power over a lifetime, assuring a steady infusion of just the right answers for difficult decisions, just the right temperament for a troublesome situation. Self-awareness involves traversing constantly shifting sands, through good weather and foul, in changing circumstances. As the Zen master Linji advised his followers: "If you meet the Buddha on the road, kill him."

We must walk on; there is more to learn, more to experience, challenges ahead to both test and deepen us. "Do not depend on the hope of results," Merton advised spiritual seekers. What we attempt, he wrote, "will be apparently worthless and even achieve no result at all, if not perhaps results opposite to what you expect. As you get used to this idea, you start more and more to concentrate not on the results but on the value, the rightness, the truth of the work itself."

The good news is that results do follow: Once consciousness becomes a practice, insight builds upon itself and feeds our progress. We do not need the accolades of the world to know that we have done something worthwhile. We know, because we know ourselves.

Take guilt, for example, the kind of anxious guilt that plagues us so that we are unable to function, unable to change the patterns that make us feel so guilty in the first place. With a healthy dose of confessional honesty and the resulting insight, we can begin to practice what I like to call "happy guilt." We acknowledge that, yes, we have committed acts we shudder to consider, but we also see that, with each day of listening to the urgings of our conscience toward goodness, we are changing. Our past lives do not represent the total person we are. All is neither lost nor gained in a day, whether it be in our most transcendent act or basest thought.

A FINAL THOUGHT

Let me leave you with this wisdom, from Paul Tillich. Tillich was not only an eminent theologian, but the kind of teacher, at Union Theological Seminary, Harvard, and the University of Chicago, to whose classes students flocked—not just for the intellectual content, but to find out how to live their lives. He often spoke of being "struck by grace."

> *We cannot transform our lives, unless we allow them to be transformed by the stroke of grace. . . . [I]t does not happen if we try to force it upon ourselves, just as it shall not happen so long as we think, in our self-complacency, that we have no need of it. Grace strikes us when we are in great pain and restlessness. It strikes us when, year after year, the longed-for perfection of life does not appear, when despair destroys all joy and courage. Sometimes at that moment a shaft of light*

breaks into our darkness, and it is as though a voice were saying, "You are accepted. You are accepted." . . . Do not try to do anything now. . . . [D]o not perform anything; do not intend anything. Simply accept the fact that you are accepted. If that happens to us, we experience grace. . . . But sometimes it happens that we receive the power to say "yes" to ourselves, that peace enters into us and makes us whole, that self-hatred and self-contempt disappear, and that our self is reunited with itself.

I wish you that grace. That you might be reunited with yourself.

BIOGRAPHY

PAUL WILKES is one of America's most respected writers and speakers on personal spirituality. Paul lectures across the country and has appeared on all major television networks and cable outlets. He has written for *The New Yorker, The Atlantic,* and *The New York Times Magazine* and is the author of a number of books, including *In Mysterious Ways: The Death and Life of a Parish Priest,* which won a Christopher Award, and most recently *In Due Season: A Catholic Life.* In addition to *Merton,* a PBS documentary, Wilkes was writer and host of the acclaimed television series *Six American Families,* which won a DuPont-Columbia Award for documentary excellence.

Paul and his wife, Tracy Wilkes, founded Homes of Hope India-US (www.homeofhopeindia.org) to assist the Home of Hope orphanage for girls in Kochi, India. He is also the cofounder of CHIPS, a Brooklyn, New York, center that has served homeless mothers and children and the poor for more than thirty-five years.

He and his wife live in Wilmington, North Carolina. Wilkes has been honored for his body of work with a Distinguished Alumnus Award from the Columbia University Graduate School of Journalism.